Phonics Practice
Made Easy and Fun

*Frustration-free method of teaching reading
to new or struggling readers*

Student Workbook B

Janis Dana

Acknowledgments
The author gratefully acknowledges the contributions and encouragement of the following individuals in the completion of this project:
Editorial: Marilee McLeod, Gail Crowley
Project Management Assistance: Kiah Dana
Cover Design Assistance: Ryan Tilly
Love and Support: Michael Dana

Dedicated to the hundreds of children who delighted me as they learned to read. It is a privilege to continue teaching through these workbooks.

Table of Contents

	Page	Check-up

Getting Started

- This is the second of two workbooks practicing 73 of the most common phonetic sounds of the English language. Workbook A is very basic, focusing on short and long vowels, consonant digraphs, and r-controlled vowels. Workbook B continues practice with other frequently encountered phonetic spellings and sounds. (See Table of Contents.)

- **Each page of *Phonics Practice Made Easy and Fun* is designed to minimize distractions and allow the learner to focus on just one sound or sound grouping at a time.** Therefore, sight words and other vocabulary have been kept to a bare minimum.

- Teach each targeted phonetic sound clearly, both verbally and in print. In the beginning, and for as long as a student needs the support, help him or her sound out and blend actual words from the worksheet containing the focus sound before starting the page. (Write them on a whiteboard or make flashcards with index cards.)

- **To keep a child from being distracted by ever-changing directions and to instill a feeling of confidence, there are only two basic formats in the worktext—and kids *love* doing them!** Before allowing independent work, walk students through lessons of both formats, teaching how to think through answers according to the directions. Do this until children thoroughly understand what they are to do.

- **Important:** Let each child freely choose two or three colors (other than black or brown) with which to complete assigned pages, thus making every page a creative expression unique to each student. It's amazing how motivating this is. Stickers or stampers may also be used for variety. If a child makes a mistake, let him X out the wrong answer and color in the right one without penalty.

- After short and long vowels, lessons can be used in order, or pick and choose to match any reading program. Faster learners will use fewer pages, but there are plenty of pages for reinforcement or homework. Note: More multi-syllabic words will be encountered in Workbook B, particularly in the Middles and Endings section.

- Use the **FIND AND FIX** feature when correcting to help prevent students from hurrying through their work without consequence for wrong answers and to provide excellent additional practice. When checking, do not mark *any wrong* on the page. Simply count the number of missed answers and record in the FIND AND FIX blank at the top left hand corner of the page. A child is then responsible for reading again through the entire page to find and fix that number of wrong answers. After doing this, if answers are still incorrect, reteach the sound and monitor the child's sounding and blending.

- Check-ups are provided after each sound or sound grouping.

- Helpful hint: Review previously practiced sounds frequently (even daily) by "chanting" their spellings and sounds with the following rhythm:

    Example for the "oy" spelling: Say the letter names "o" and "y" twice, then the sound three times: o - y, o – y, /oy/, /oy/, /oy/. This can be done with all the letter combinations. Great technique for cementing each sound and spelling into the mind.

Name_____

Directions for the student: **Practice reading 16 short ea words on this page.** Choose 2-3 colors. Color *yes* if the sentence makes sense or could possibly be true. Color *no* if it does not make sense or could not be true.

1. The bread read to me. | yes | no |

2. Do this instead of that. | yes | no |

3. A head is made of lead. | yes | no |

4. Dead men fix sweaters. | yes | no |

5. A feather is heavy. | yes | no |

6. Heather dreads the test. | yes | no |

7. A sock is wealthy. | yes | no |

8. Mix breath in the bread. | yes | no |

9. Thread can mend a rip. | yes | no |

10. A dog has feathers. | yes | no |

Name_____

Directions for the student: **Practice reading 21 short ea words on this page.** Choose 2-3 colors. Read each sentence or phrase. Pick the best answer and color it.

1. Heather bit into it.

feather	bread

2. Not sick

healthy	wealthy

3. This, not that

read	instead

4. On your neck

lead	head

5. A gun

read	weapon

6. It can smell bad.

breath	instead

7. Let's go!

ready	head

8. Fix a rip with it.

wealth	thread

9. Can't pick it up.

heavy	healthy

10. A mint is for it.

breath	sweater

Name_____

Directions for the student: **Practice reading 16 short ea words on this page.** Choose 2-3 colors. Color *yes* if the sentence makes sense or could possibly be true. Color *no* if it does not make sense or could not be true.

1. Thread is heavy. | yes | no |

2. Pigs mend sweaters. | yes | no |

3. Socks are for heads. | yes | no |

4. He has a leather belt. | yes | no |

5. A feather is a weapon. | yes | no |

6. I am ready for bed. | yes | no |

7. Spread sweat on bread. | yes | no |

8. I dread bad weather. | yes | no |

9. A dog has feathers. | yes | no |

10. Heather is wealthy. | yes | no |

Name_____

Directions for the student: **Practice reading 23 short ea words on this page.** Choose 2-3 colors. Read each sentence or phrase. Pick the best answer and color it.

1. It can be red.

head	thread

2. A fat man

heavy	read

3. Belts can be this.

leather	weather

4. Had a last breath

lead	dead

5. He had eggs for it.

wealth	breakfast

6. It fits Heather.

feather	sweater

7. Do it if hot.

deaf	sweat

8. Spread jam on it.

health	bread

9. A hat is on it.

head	health

10. Soft

instead	feather

4

Name_____

Directions for the student: **Practice reading 15 short ea words on this page.** Choose 2-3 colors. Color **yes** if the sentence makes sense or could possibly be true. Color **no** if it does not make sense or could not be true.

1. I meant to get thread. | yes | no |

2. A cat has feathers. | yes | no |

3. Candy is healthy. | yes | no |

4. A pen has lead in it. | yes | no |

5. Heather read to him. | yes | no |

6. I'm ready for the weather. | yes | no |

7. A deaf kid had bread. | yes | no |

8. Drop the weapon! | yes | no |

9. My head will snap off. | yes | no |

10. A dead man has breath. | yes | no |

Name_____

Directions for the student: **Practice reading 22 short ea words on this page.** Choose 2-3 colors. Read each sentence or phrase. Pick the best answer and color it.

1. A sandwich has it.	instead	bread
2. It is on his head.	wealth	sweat
3. Rocks can be it.	heavy	thread
4. It can be hot.	weather	read
5. Planned to	meant	breath
6. Afraid to see it	thread	dread
7. Has a skull.	heavy	head
8. Can kill.	weapon	feather
9. After the last breath	death	sweat
10. Dan's jacket	breath	leather

Name_____

Directions for the student: Color **yes** if the sentence makes sense or could possibly be true. Color **no** if it does not make sense or could not be true.

1. Bread sweats.

yes	no

2. Feathers get deaf.

yes	no

3. Thread can be red.

yes	no

4. He has a leather head.

yes	no

5. My sweater is dead.

yes	no

Directions for the student: Read each sentence or phrase. Pick the best answer and color it.

6. Man with no breath

dead	read

7. A lot to spend

meant	wealth

8. Not heavy

feather	lead

9. It can smell bad.

thread	sweat

10. Heather did it.

read	deaf

Name_____

Directions for the student: **Practice reading 22 ie words on this page.** Choose 2-3 colors. Color *yes* if the sentence makes sense or could possibly be true. Color *no* if it does not make sense or could not be true.

1. My niece believes Evie.

yes	no

2. Alfie had a piece of cake.

yes	no

3. Sad Debbie felt grief.

yes	no

4. Rosie had a brief nap.

yes	no

5. Brownies grow in fields.

yes	no

6. Baby Alfie lost a bootie.

yes	no

7. A thief hid in the field.

yes	no

8. A priest believes in God.

yes	no

9. Annie ate Ellie's cookie.

yes	no

10. Eddie ate his niece.

yes	no

Name_____

Directions for the student: **Practice reading 22 ie words on this page.** Choose 2-3 colors. Read each sentence or phrase. Pick the best answer and color it.

1. He robs.

grief	thief

2. Go run in it.

field	believe

3. His job is in church.

thief	priest

4. Quick

brief	field

5. Cut a piece of it.

priest	brownie

6. A girl

field	niece

7. Sadness

thief	grief

8. To trust

believe	field

9. Evie had six.

chief	cookies

10. Baby Annie's sock

bootie	yield

10

ei and eigh (as in v**ei**n and sl**eigh**)

Name_____

Directions for the student: **Practice reading 17 ei / eigh words on this page.** Choose 2-3 colors. Color *yes* if the sentence makes sense or could possibly be true. Color *no* if it does not make sense or could not be true.

1. Santa is in his sleigh. | yes | no |

2. Eight kids lost their veins. | yes | no |

3. The freight train is late. | yes | no |

4. Bugs weigh a lot. | yes | no |

5. A king rules and reigns. | yes | no |

6. The bride wore a veil. | yes | no |

7. Their weight went up. | yes | no |

8. Veins cost eighty bucks. | yes | no |

9. We see eighteen reindeer. | yes | no |

10. Their neighbor is eighty. | yes | no |

ei and eigh (as in vein and sleigh)

Name_____

Directions for the student: **Practice reading 21 ei / eigh words on this page.** Choose 2-3 colors. Read each sentence or phrase. Pick the best answer and color it.

1. A bride has it on.

sleigh	veil

2. It is after seven.

eight	vein

3. Do it on a scale.

freight	weigh

4. He is next door.

neighbor	veil

5. Under the skin

veins	weigh

6. A load for trains

freight	reigns

7. It will go in snow.

weigh	sleigh

8. For a horse

veil	reigns

9. Can gain it.

vein	weight

10. In front of a sleigh

reindeer	eighty

12

Name_____

Directions for the student: **Practice reading 10 ei words on this page.** Choose 2-3 colors. Color *yes* if the sentence makes sense or could possibly be true. Color *no* if it does not make sense or could not be true.

1. We run on the ceiling.

yes	no

2. Get a receipt for the gas.

yes	no

3. Conceited girls brag.

yes	no

4. A tree deceived me.

yes	no

5. I perceive it's the truth.

yes	no

6. We conceived a plan.

yes	no

7. A pond has a ceiling.

yes	no

8. "Deceit" is to hide truth.

yes	no

9. I received a letter.

yes	no

10. Cats give out receipts.

yes	no

Name_____

Directions for the student: **Practice reading 20 ei words on this page.** Choose 2-3 colors. Read each sentence or phrase. Pick the best answer and color it.

1. Brags she's best

receipt	conceited

2. Lies to you

perceive	deceives

3. Get what's given

ceiling	receive

4. A brain can do it.

conceive	receipt

5. From a store

receipt	deceit

6. It needs paint.

conceit	ceiling

7. Not as it seems

deceit	receive

8. A slip of paper

receipt	perceive

9. To think up

conceive	deceive

10. A room has it.

conceit	ceiling

14

Name_____

Directions for the student: **Practice reading 27 ie / ei / eigh words on this page.** Choose 2-3 colors. Color *yes* if the sentence makes sense or could possibly be true. Color *no* if it does not make sense or could not be true.

1. I believe Josie's neighbor. | yes | no |

2. My niece Ellie lost weight. | yes | no |

3. A thief stole their ceiling. | yes | no |

4. Julie's veins believe you. | yes | no |

5. Millie did rip Annie's veil. | yes | no |

6. Their priest is eighty. | yes | no |

7. Thieves weigh pigs. | yes | no |

8. My auntie's niece is eight. | yes | no |

9. Eat a piece of the sleigh. | yes | no |

10. I will deceive the field. | yes | no |

Name_____

Directions for the student: **Practice reading 30 ie / ei / eigh words on this page.** Choose 2-3 colors. Read each sentence or phrase. Pick the best answer and color it.

1. Debbie ate eight.

grief	cookies

2. Help Alfie fix it.

ceiling	field

3. Eat to gain weight.

brownies	thief

4. To trick

deceive	conceit

5. Do not believe him.

auntie	thief

6. Get a receipt for it.

veil	goalie

7. Neighbors go here.

cutie	movies

8. Ten plus eight

eighteen	priest

9. Maggie had it on.

nightie	field

10. Annie got in it.

receive	sleigh

ie / cei and **ei / eigh** (as in gr**ie**f / de**cei**t and v**ei**n / sl**eigh**)

Name_____

Directions for the student: **Practice reading 25 ie / ei / eigh words on this page.** Choose 2-3 colors. Color *yes* if the sentence makes sense or could possibly be true. Color *no* if it does not make sense or could not be true.

1. Millie ate eight brownies. | yes | no |

2. Debbie believes the priest. | yes | no |

3. A thief deceived Billie. | yes | no |

4. Neighbors sit on ceilings. | yes | no |

5. Annie bent Julie's veins. | yes | no |

6. My niece is a reindeer. | yes | no |

7. A bride wore eighty veils. | yes | no |

8. Josie's auntie is conceited. | yes | no |

9. I perceive he lost weight. | yes | no |

10. Zombies ride in sleighs. | yes | no |

ie / cei and ei / eigh (as in grief / deceit and vein / sleigh)

Name_____

Directions for the student: **Practice reading 30 ie / ei / eigh words on this page.** Choose 2-3 colors. Read each sentence or phrase. Pick the best answer and color it.

1. Lock him up.	veins	thief
2. He will help us.	neighbor	conceit
3. Maggie lost it.	priest	receipt
4. Katie went here.	their	movies
5. An old man's age	ceiling	eighty
6. To mislead	deceive	nightie
7. Sandie's dog	Lassie	reigns
8. Ship it.	conceive	freight
9. To get from him	receive	field
10. A number	veil	eight

Name_____

Directions for the student: Color **yes** if the sentence makes sense or could possibly be true. Color **no** if it does not make sense or could not be true.

1. I believe babies smoke. | yes | no |

2. Eight kids bit their feet. | yes | no |

3. Annie ran on a ceiling. | yes | no |

4. Their weight went up. | yes | no |

5. My neighbor has a niece. | yes | no |

Directions for the student: Read each sentence or phrase. Pick the best answer and color it.

6. Quick | veins | brief |

7. After seven | piece | eight |

8. My niece kept it. | receipt | yield |

9. A bride may have it. | veil | thief |

10. To not tell the truth | deceive | reigns |

Name_____

Directions for the student: **Practice reading 18 oi words on this page.** Choose 2-3 colors. Color *yes* if the sentence makes sense or could possibly be true. Color *no* if it does not make sense or could not be true.

1. Boil foil in the toilet.	yes	no
2. Al will join the club.	yes	no
3. Plant it in moist soil.	yes	no
4. Coins oink.	yes	no
5. That toilet made noise.	yes	no
6. Oil can drip.	yes	no
7. Avoid poison.	yes	no
8. We boil noise.	yes	no
9. A pin has a point.	yes	no
10. Spoil the coin.	yes	no

Name_____

Directions for the student: **Practice reading 20 oi words on this page.** Choose 2-3 colors. Read each sentence or phrase. Pick the best answer and color it.

1. A hand can do it.

point	oink

2. Flush it.

coil	toilet

3. A car needs it.

foil	oil

4. A bit wet

noise	moist

5. Plant seeds in it.

soil	poison

6. To make tea *hot.*

coil	boil

7. A dime

coin	foil

8. Do not eat it!

noise	poison

9. To get into a club

join	moist

10. Kids make it.

noise	soil

22

Name_____

Directions for the student: **Practice reading 13 oi words on this page.** Choose 2-3 colors. Color *yes* if the sentence makes sense or could possibly be true. Color *no* if it does not make sense or could not be true.

1. Point to the coins.

yes	no

2. Dad got oil for his van.

yes	no

3. We boil toilets.

yes	no

4. Mom will get the foil.

yes	no

5. Pigs oink.

yes	no

6. Hens join hands.

yes	no

7. Kids sip poison.

yes	no

8. The sun is moist.

yes	no

9. We oil soil.

yes	no

10. Six kids sit on a toilet.

yes	no

Name_____

Directions for the student: **Practice reading 20 oi words on this page.** Choose 2-3 colors. Read each sentence or phrase. Pick the best answer and color it.

1. It can kill you.

toilet	poison

2. Damp

moist	noise

3. A kid can drop it.

join	coin

4. Do it in a pan.

boil	coil

5. Plants need it.

noise	soil

6. Spend them.

oil	coins

7. It drips from old vans.

soil	oil

8. It can smell bad.

join	toilet

9. Hit drums to make it.

noise	foil

10. On the end of a pin

coil	point

24

Name_____

Directions for the student: **Practice reading 11 oi words on this page.** Choose 2-3 colors. Color **yes** if the sentence makes sense or could possibly be true. Color **no** if it does not make sense or could not be true.

1. I spent the coin.

yes	no

2. Apes use a toilet.

yes	no

3. Oil the kids.

yes	no

4. We made noise.

yes	no

5. I will boil the soil.

yes	no

6. The cake is moist.

yes	no

7. We will join hands.

yes	no

8. Broil the ham.

yes	no

9. Milk is poison.

yes	no

10. I will point at him.

yes	no

Name_____

Directions for the student: **Practice reading 20 oi words on this page.** Choose 2-3 colors. Read each sentence or phrase. Pick the best answer and color it.

1. It can cover a dish.

joint	foil

2. Mom can't stand it.

noise	join

3. A snake will do it.

point	coil

4. Can hear it.

voice	oil

5. Do it to hot dogs.

boil	coin

6. Milk can do it.

spoil	voice

7. A leg bends here.

joint	broil

8. Save them.

oink	coins

9. Sit on it and go.

voice	toilet

10. Lock it up.

poison	noise

26

Name_____

Directions for the student: Color **yes** if the sentence makes sense or could possibly be true. Color **no** if it does not make sense or could not be true.

1. Poison oinks.

yes	no

2. Boil the toilet.

yes	no

3. Point at the coins.

yes	no

4. Join us on a trip.

yes	no

5. Moist soil makes noise.

yes	no

Directions for the student: Read each sentence or phrase. Pick the best answer and color it.

6. Can be on a dish

foil	join

7. Ed has a lot of them.

oil	coins

8. Dig in it.

soil	broil

9. Can get you sick

noise	poison

10. A pig's voice

joint	oink

Name_____

Directions for the student: **Practice reading 15 oy words on this page.** Choose 2-3 colors. Color *yes* if the sentence makes sense or could possibly be true. Color *no* if it does not make sense or could not be true.

1. A dress is for a boy. | yes | no |

2. Joy has toys. | yes | no |

3. Roy's dog is loyal. | yes | no |

4. Kids enjoy sores. | yes | no |

5. Fire can destroy homes. | yes | no |

6. Floyd's cat annoys me. | yes | no |

7. The royal queen is here. | yes | no |

8. To employ is to hire. | yes | no |

9. Toys are just for boys. | yes | no |

10. Troy will fix Boyd's van. | yes | no |

Name_____

Directions for the student: **Practice reading 21 oy words on this page.** Choose 2-3 colors. Read each sentence or phrase. Pick the best answer and color it.

1. Happy, happy!

destroy	joy

2. Roy plays with them.

soy	toys

3. Nag, nag, nag

joy	annoy

4. Pay to do a job

voyage	employ

5. A queen is this.

royal	toy

6. Not a girl

soy	boy

7. A doll

destroy	toy

8. Will stick by you

loyal	royal

9. A kind of bean

toy	soy

10. To crash and smash

Joy	destroy

Name_____

Directions for the student: **Practice reading 18 oy words on this page.** Choose 2-3 colors. Color *yes* if the sentence makes sense or could possibly be true. Color *no* if it does not make sense or could not be true.

1. Joy is a tomboy. | yes | no |

2. Roy enjoys math. | yes | no |

3. Toys destroy boys. | yes | no |

4. A sock has joy. | yes | no |

5. Maps annoy cats. | yes | no |

6. Floyd will nap. | yes | no |

7. Boyd is loyal to Troy. | yes | no |

8. We will destroy the sun. | yes | no |

9. Roy enjoys trips. | yes | no |

10. A joyful boy is happy. | yes | no |

oy (as in b**oy**)

Name_____

Directions for the student: **Practice reading 24 oy words on this page.** Choose 2-3 colors. Read each sentence or phrase. Pick the best answer and color it.

1. To bother

annoy	toy

2. Troy, Floyd, and Roy

soy	boys

3. Pay to do a job

employ	destroy

4. A big trip

voyage	loyal

5. She acts like a boy.

enjoy	tomboy

6. Always helps

annoy	loyal

7. To like something

employ	enjoy

8. To wipe out

soy	destroy

9. A game

toy	boy

10. To be so glad

joyful	annoy

32

Name_____

Directions for the student: **Practice reading 16 oy words on this page.** Choose 2-3 colors. Color *yes* if the sentence makes sense or could possibly be true. Color *no* if it does not make sense or could not be true.

1. The boys annoy Troy. | yes | no |

2. Roy destroys his toy. | yes | no |

3. Joy is joyful. | yes | no |

4. We enjoy bad smells. | yes | no |

5. Pins are loyal. | yes | no |

6. It was a fun voyage. | yes | no |

7. Boyd lost his toy. | yes | no |

8. Do not annoy Dad. | yes | no |

9. We enjoy gifts. | yes | no |

10. Floyd slept. | yes | no |

Name_____

Directions for the student: **Practice reading 21 oy words on this page.** Choose 2-3 colors. Read each sentence or phrase. Pick the best answer and color it.

1. To hire | enjoy | employ

2. Grow up to be dads | toys | boys

3. To crash a car | destroy | loyal

4. Happy to do it | royal | enjoy

5. Can't stand it | enjoy | annoy

6. Joy's twin | soy | Roy

7. A gift for a kid | royal | toy

8. Stays by your side | destroy | loyal

9. It can take weeks. | voyage | annoy

10. Not sad | royal | joyful

Name_____

Directions for the student: Color **yes** if the sentence makes sense or could possibly be true. Color **no** if it does not make sense or could not be true.

1. Toys annoy kids.

yes	no

2. Joy's dog enjoys bones.

yes	no

3. Bad boys destroy toys.

yes	no

4. The gift gave Roy joy.

yes	no

5. Rocks annoy weeds.

yes	no

Directions for the student: Read each sentence or phrase. Pick the best answer and color it.

6. To like a lot

enjoy	annoy

7. For kids

toys	royal

8. A ship can go on it.

voyage	soy

9. Queens and kings

royalty	boys

10. Fire can do it.

loyal	destroy

Name_____

Directions for the student: **Practice reading 20 ow words on this page.** Choose 2-3 colors. Color *yes* if the sentence makes sense or could possibly be true. Color *no* if it does not make sense or could not be true.

1. Flowers have power. | yes | no |

2. Owls growl at cows. | yes | no |

3. The clown sat down. | yes | no |

4. The drowsy man naps. | yes | no |

5. Get me a brown towel. | yes | no |

6. A crowd is downtown. | yes | no |

7. The crown is gold. | yes | no |

8. Cows bow down to pigs. | yes | no |

9. Mom frowns at me. | yes | no |

10. Jan's gown is brown. | yes | no |

Name_____

Directions for the student: **Practice reading 21 ow words on this page.** Choose 2-3 colors. Read each sentence or phrase. Pick the best answer and color it.

1. Not up
crown	down

2. To die under water
drown	brown

3. Dry with it.
town	towel

4. Not later
now	how

5. You do it, if sad.
frown	plow

6. An owl can be it.
brow	brown

7. A dog may do it.
gown	growl

8. On a queen
crown	owl

9. Milk it.
crowd	cow

10. A rose
down	flower

ow (as in **ow**l)

Name_____

Directions for the student: **Practice reading 19 ow words on this page.** Choose 2-3 colors. Color *yes* if the sentence makes sense or could possibly be true. Color *no* if it does not make sense or could not be true.

1. Owls nap in gowns. | yes | no |

2. The crowd yells. | yes | no |

3. Flowers growl and howl. | yes | no |

4. That towel is brown. | yes | no |

5. A crown is for a queen. | yes | no |

6. Cows allow us to frown. | yes | no |

7. Feet now have brows. | yes | no |

8. Bow down to the king. | yes | no |

9. An owl drowns in a tree. | yes | no |

10. Mom allows us to go. | yes | no |

Name_____

Directions for the student: **Practice reading 20 ow words on this page.** Choose 2-3 colors. Read each sentence or phrase. Pick the best answer and color it.

1. He can do tricks.

brown	clown

2. Lips do it.

frown	town

3. Gets you wet

towel	shower

4. At this time

now	gown

5. Skin can be this.

brown	growl

6. On a castle

tower	drown

7. Sits in a tree

cow	owl

8. A long dress

gown	crown

9. Let him.

flower	allow

10. A truck can do it.

down	plow

Name_____

Directions for the student: **Practice reading 17 ow words on this page.** Choose 2-3 colors. Color *yes* if the sentence makes sense or could possibly be true. Color *no* if it does not make sense or could not be true.

1. Flowers need towels. | yes | no |

2. Clowns growl at owls. | yes | no |

3. A tree can drown. | yes | no |

4. Plow the brown soil. | yes | no |

5. Go downtown. | yes | no |

6. Cows like gowns. | yes | no |

7. Owls take showers. | yes | no |

8. Allow me to help. | yes | no |

9. A bug has lots of power. | yes | no |

10. His vest is brown. | yes | no |

Name_____

Directions for the student: **Practice reading 21 ow words on this page.** Choose 2-3 colors. Read each sentence or phrase. Pick the best answer and color it.

1. It can be brown.

allow	towel

2. Sleepy

frown	drowsy

3. It eats grass.

cow	growl

4. To permit

growl	allow

5. Can turn it on or off.

power	tower

6. Ann picks them.

flowers	brown

7. It is a bird.

cow	owl

8. A girl has it on.

gown	now

9. A lot of people

flower	crowd

10. A princess had it on.

crown	town

Name_____

Directions for the student: Color **yes** if the sentence makes sense or could possibly be true. Color **no** if it does not make sense or could not be true.

1. Clowns milk cows.	yes	no
2. A towel howls.	yes	no
3. Drown the frown.	yes	no
4. Allow him to shower.	yes	no
5. Sit down now.	yes	no

Directions for the student: Read each sentence or phrase. Pick the best answer and color it.

6. Ask it.	how	power
7. Smell them.	flowers	towns
8. Lips that go down	brow	frown
9. Pants can be it	crown	brown
10. A time	now	gown

Name_____

Directions for the student: **Practice reading 22 ou words on this page.** Choose 2-3 colors. Color *yes* if the sentence makes sense or could possibly be true. Color *no* if it does not make sense or could not be true.

1. A house shouts out loud. | yes | no |

2. Al is a grouch. | yes | no |

3. Get a pound of flour. | yes | no |

4. A mouse counts clouds. | yes | no |

5. I slept about an hour. | yes | no |

6. Our couch is proud. | yes | no |

7. A bus is round. | yes | no |

8. Flour is sour. | yes | no |

9. A mouth can pout. | yes | no |

10. A blouse fits a mouse. | yes | no |

FIND AND FIX _____   ou (as in out)

Name_____

Directions for the student: **Practice reading 22 ou words on this page.** Choose 2-3 colors. Read each sentence or phrase. Pick the best answer and color it.

1. Like a rat

round	mouse

2. Sit on it.

house	couch

3. Can do it to nails

mouth	pound

4. I sleep here.

cloud	house

5. Ham can be in it.

mouth	loud

6. It is in the sky.

ground	cloud

7. A globe is this.

round	pound

8. It can be loud.

found	sound

9. How I can feel

proud	mouth

10. It is our Mom's.

loud	blouse

Name_____

Directions for the student: **Practice reading 21 ou words on this page.** Choose 2-3 colors. Color **yes** if the sentence makes sense or could possibly be true. Color **no** if it does not make sense or could not be true.

1. Bounce the house. | yes | no |

2. Mom is proud of me. | yes | no |

3. A grouch may pout. | yes | no |

4. I found my lost mouth. | yes | no |

5. A mouse is so loud! | yes | no |

6. Our couch can count. | yes | no |

7. A blouse yells out loud. | yes | no |

8. Clouds are round. | yes | no |

9. Our house is big. | yes | no |

10. The ground is sour. | yes | no |

Name_____

Directions for the student: **Practice reading 22 ou words on this page.** Choose 2-3 colors. Read each sentence or phrase. Pick the best answer and color it.

1. Not a soft sound	loud	cloud
2. 1, 2, 3, …	scout	count
3. Feel good about it.	pound	proud
4. I can dig in it.	ground	cloud
5. Not sweet	sour	loud
6. A pinch on my skin	couch	ouch
7. Not in	round	out
8. It can smile.	house	mouth
9. Up by the sun	cloud	pout
10. Not lost	mouse	found

Name_____

Directions for the student: **Practice reading 21 ou words on this page.** Choose 2-3 colors. Color *yes* if the sentence makes sense or could possibly be true. Color *no* if it does not make sense or could not be true.

1. A couch has a mouth. | yes | no |

2. Pound the cloud. | yes | no |

3. A house is round. | yes | no |

4. I found out about him. | yes | no |

5. Tell our dad about it. | yes | no |

6. Step out on the cloud. | yes | no |

7. Bounce the mouse. | yes | no |

8. I found a pouch. | yes | no |

9. Her blouse can count. | yes | no |

10. Get out of the house. | yes | no |

ou (as in **out**)

Name_____

Directions for the student: **Practice reading 21 ou words on this page.** Choose 2-3 colors. Read each sentence or phrase. Pick the best answer and color it.

1. Fluffy and white

cloud	proud

2. It is a home.

house	south

3. Grass is on it.

sound	ground

4. Ours is brown.

grouch	couch

5. It scared Mom.

house	mouse

6. Thunder

loud	pouch

7. It hurts!

round	ouch

8. Open it wide!

mouth	count

9. A lemon

noun	sour

10. Button it up.

blouse	pound

Name_____

Directions for the student: Color **yes** if the sentence makes sense or could possibly be true. Color **no** if it does not make sense or could not be true.

1. Mom found her blouse. | yes | no

2. Go out for an hour. | yes | no

3. Dan shouts, "Ouch!" | yes | no

4. A cloud is made of flour. | yes | no

5. A mouse can count. | yes | no

Directions for the student: Read each sentence or phrase. Pick the best answer and color it.

6. Step on it. | ground | sound

7. To scrub | sour | scour

8. See it up, up, up | house | cloud

9. I got a spot on it. | south | blouse

10. To hit a nail | pound | noun

ough (as in thou**ght**, d**ough**, thr**ough**, r**ough**, c**ough**, and b**ough**)

Name_____

Directions for the student: **Practice reading 11 ough words on this page.** Choose 2-3 colors. Color **yes** if the sentence makes sense or could possibly be true. Color **no** if it does not make sense or could not be true.

1. I thought he was through. | yes | no |

2. Make ham from dough. | yes | no |

3. Mom brought me milk. | yes | no |

4. A tree and a pig fought. | yes | no |

5. I ate enough. | yes | no |

6. I had a bad cough. | yes | no |

7. My cat bought a hat. | yes | no |

8. This meat is tough. | yes | no |

9. Though I try, I can't. | yes | no |

10. A rock can feel rough. | yes | no |

Name_____

Directions for the student: **Practice reading 20 ough words on this page.** Choose 2-3 colors. Read each sentence or phrase. Pick the best answer and color it.

1. In my mind

brought	thought

2. Not smooth

rough	though

3. Mix it.

dough	fought

4. Got it at a store

bought	tough

5. Even if

fought	though

6. Did bring it

brought	cough

7. Go in, then out.

rough	through

8. No more

enough	sought

9. Did fight

dough	fought

10. May do it if sick

cough	rough

Name_____

Directions for the student: **Practice reading 12 ough words on this page.** Choose 2-3 colors. Color *yes* if the sentence makes sense or could possibly be true. Color *no* if it does not make sense or could not be true.

1. Silk feels rough.

yes	no

2. Go through the papers.

yes	no

3. I thought I bought you.

yes	no

4. Dad got rid of his cough.

yes	no

5. I made enough dough.

yes	no

6. The tree's bough fell.

yes	no

7. Rocks ought to sleep.

yes	no

8. I brought him a gift.

yes	no

9. We fought and won.

yes	no

10. I'm through with this.

yes	no

Name_____

Directions for the student: **Practice reading 21 ough words on this page.** Choose 2-3 colors. Read each sentence or phrase. Pick the best answer and color it.

1. Not enough rain

cough	drought

2. Tree branch

sought	bough

3. Way to spell plow

rough	plough

4. Hard to bite meat

tough	thought

5. Plenty

sought	enough

6. Paid for it

bought	cough

7. In Al's brain

thought	ought

8. Finished

through	rough

9. I ate it.

doughnut	drought

10. Tried to find

sought	tough

Name_____

Directions for the student: **Practice reading 11 ough words on this page.** Choose 2-3 colors. Color *yes* if the sentence makes sense or could possibly be true. Color *no* if it does not make sense or could not be true.

1. A leg has thoughts. | yes | no |

2. It was a tough test. | yes | no |

3. The pig brought us tea. | yes | no |

4. We had enough rain. | yes | no |

5. The brats fought. | yes | no |

6. A rock sought to find me. | yes | no |

7. We bought a sled. | yes | no |

8. Doughnuts cough. | yes | no |

9. I act as though I'm sick. | yes | no |

10. A drought can be bad. | yes | no |

Name_____

Directions for the student: **Practice reading 20 ough words on this page.** Choose 2-3 colors. Read each sentence or phrase. Pick the best answer and color it.

1. All that we need

enough	ought

2. Roll it out.

thought	dough

3. Ed can't help it.

cough	sought

4. Done with dinner

rough	through

5. Dry, dry weather

drought	enough

6. Needs to

ought	rough

7. Carried with me

brought	ought

8. Bumpy and choppy

thought	rough

9. Hunted for it

sought	drought

10. Got with money

though	bought

58

Name_____

Directions for the student: Color **yes** if the sentence makes sense or could possibly be true. Color **no** if it does not make sense or could not be true.

1. I thought he brought it. | yes | no |

2. Dough can cough. | yes | no |

3. He bought enough cups. | yes | no |

4. We ran through the sun. | yes | no |

5. I went, although I'm sick. | yes | no |

Directions for the student: Read each sentence or phrase. Pick the best answer and color it.

6. I am finished. | through | though |

7. Got it with cash | brought | bought |

8. Did think | drought | thought |

9. All that we need | enough | rough |

10. Even though | cough | although |

Name_____

Directions for the student: **Practice reading 20 oo words on this page.** Choose 2-3 colors. Color **yes** if the sentence makes sense or could possibly be true. Color **no** if it does not make sense or could not be true.

1. I will sit on a stool, too. | yes | no |

2. Boots drool. | yes | no |

3. Let's go to the zoo soon. | yes | no |

4. Roosters sit on spoons. | yes | no |

5. A goose will say, "Moo". | yes | no |

6. We cool off in a pool. | yes | no |

7. The moon will shoot us. | yes | no |

8. A tool is in his room. | yes | no |

9. Grooms ride brooms. | yes | no |

10. A moose hoots. | yes | no |

Name_____

Directions for the student: **Practice reading 24 oo words on this page.** Choose 2-3 colors. Read each sentence or phrase. Pick the best answer and color it.

1. Swim in it.	broom	pool
2. Can get loose	zoo	tooth
3. A time	shoot	noon
4. It shines.	hoot	moon
5. A stool can be in it.	room	hoot
6. See a moose here.	cool	zoo
7. Eat it with a spoon.	fool	food
8. Do it with a gun	shoot	snooze
9. Not hot	cool	boot
10. To pick	choose	zoo

Name_____

Directions for the student: **Practice reading 20 oo words on this page.** Choose 2-3 colors. Color **yes** if the sentence makes sense or could possibly be true. Color **no** if it does not make sense or could not be true.

1. Ed snoops in Al's room. | yes | no |

2. The hot food will cool. | yes | no |

3. Choose the red balloon. | yes | no |

4. Shoot the food. | yes | no |

5. Spoons toot. | yes | no |

6. The boot has a tooth. | yes | no |

7. A broom hoots. | yes | no |

8. Snooze in your room. | yes | no |

9. Scoop up the moon. | yes | no |

10. Poop is food. | yes | no |

Name_____

Directions for the student: **Practice reading 24 oo words on this page.** Choose 2-3 colors. Read each sentence or phrase. Pick the best answer and color it.

1. It gets dust up.

food	broom

2. To nap a bit

snooze	toot

3. Cool off in it.

hoot	pool

4. Time for lunch

noon	moon

5. It smells!

tooth	poop

6. See them on feet.

boots	pools

7. In a little bit

soon	room

8. On a bib

drool	stool

9. Scoop food with it.

spoon	hoop

10. Dan's is loose.

booth	tooth

Name_____

Directions for the student: **Practice reading 21 oo words on this page.** Choose 2-3 colors. Color **yes** if the sentence makes sense or could possibly be true. Color **no** if it does not make sense or could not be true.

1. I took the books home. | yes | no |

2. He stood in the brook. | yes | no |

3. Look for the cook. | yes | no |

4. A crook took my foot. | yes | no |

5. Mom cooks wood. | yes | no |

6. I shook my hood. | yes | no |

7. Dad took a look at me. | yes | no |

8. Jan stood on the wood. | yes | no |

9. Dan took a cookie. | yes | no |

10. Get me a cookbook. | yes | no |

Name_____

Directions for the student: **Practice reading 25 oo words on this page.** Choose 2-3 colors. Read each sentence or phrase. Pick the best answer and color it.

1. Mom will do it.

foot	cook

2. A cook can look at it.

took	book

3. A desk

brook	wood

4. Ken took it.

cookie	stood

5. A wet dog did it.

cook	shook

6. On a jacket

hood	crook

7. To see

look	hook

8. I did it on a step.

stood	hood

9. From a tree

cook	wood

10. He took the books.

crook	foot

Name_____

Directions for the student: **Practice reading 21 oo words on this page.** Choose 2-3 colors. Color **yes** if the sentence makes sense or could possibly be true. Color **no** if it does not make sense or could not be true.

1. My cookbook got wet. | yes | no |

2. Look at my foot. | yes | no |

3. The crook took the gold. | yes | no |

4. Mom is a good cook. | yes | no |

5. This book is good. | yes | no |

6. I shook the brook. | yes | no |

7. My hood is on the hook. | yes | no |

8. The cook took the pan. | yes | no |

9. Cook cookies in a brook. | yes | no |

10. The hood stood up. | yes | no |

Name_____

Directions for the student: **Practice reading 22 oo words on this page.** Choose 2-3 colors. Read each sentence or phrase. Pick the best answer and color it.

1. Not bad

good	took

2. A cold dog did it.

crook	shook

3. Look for it on a shelf.

book	brook

4. A hat on a jacket

hood	cook

5. A sock is on it.

hook	foot

6. Got up.

brook	stood

7. A cook bakes it.

cookie	took

8. Ted's hat is on it.

hook	book

9. He robs a shop.

crook	stood

10. Fish swim in it.

brook	wood

Name_____

Directions for the student: **Practice reading 23 oo words on this page.** Choose 2-3 colors. Color **yes** if the sentence makes sense or could possibly be true. Color **no** if it does not make sense or could not be true.

1. His foot lost a tooth. | yes | no |

2. A crook took his roof. | yes | no |

3. Wood drools. | yes | no |

4. The groom looks good. | yes | no |

5. I stood on a wood stool. | yes | no |

6. The moon is on a hook. | yes | no |

7. A goose cooks. | yes | no |

8. Stick a foot in the pool. | yes | no |

9. Ben took Dan's boot. | yes | no |

10. Poop is in the bathroom. | yes | no |

oo (as in **zoo** and **book**)

Name_____

Directions for the student: **Practice reading 21 oo words on this page.** Choose 2-3 colors. Read each sentence or phrase. Pick the best answer and color it.

1. A fan helps do it.

hood	cool

2. An ax can cut it.

drool	wood

3. Swim in it.

pool	book

4. He gets a wife.

groom	hood

5. To go fast

foot	zoom

6. Not bad

good	moose

7. Mom did it to a rug.

shook	moon

8. It can get a fish.

hook	fool

9. Need tools to fix it.

roof	book

10. Do it with pans.

crook	cook

Name_____

Directions for the student: Color **yes** if the sentence makes sense or could possibly be true. Color **no** if it does not make sense or could not be true.

1. A crook took the moon.

yes	no

2. I took the tools home.

yes	no

3. She looks cool.

yes	no

4. Books swim in pools.

yes	no

5. Cook the boots.

yes	no

Directions for the student: Read each sentence or phrase. Pick the best answer and color it.

6. Ed put his ___ on.

hoot	hood

7. A jet can do it.

foot	zoom

8. Sit on it.

hook	stool

9. Dogs can do it.

cook	drool

10. I got it as a gift.

book	fool

Name_____

Directions for the student: **Practice reading 14 aw words on this page.** Choose 2-3 colors. Color *yes* if the sentence makes sense or could possibly be true. Color *no* if it does not make sense or could not be true.

1. The beef is raw.

yes	no

2. Kids lick paws.

yes	no

3. I saw Dawn yawn.

yes	no

4. Sip milk with a straw.

yes	no

5. Mom got up at dawn.

yes	no

6. Dad will cut the lawn.

yes	no

7. He hit my jaw.

yes	no

8. Crawl on the sun.

yes	no

9. Ed can draw a hawk.

yes	no

10. Shawn broke the law.

yes	no

Name_____

Directions for the student: **Practice reading 20 aw words on this page.** Choose 2-3 colors. Read each sentence or phrase. Pick the best answer and color it.

1. On a cat | saw | paws |

2. Sip with it. | straw | lawn |

3. A baby will do it. | claw | crawl |

4. The sun will go up. | dawn | fawn |

5. Do it with a pen. | draw | dawn |

6. A chin | raw | jaw |

7. It can cut. | straw | saw |

8. On a bird | raw | claw |

9. You do it if tired. | yawn | law |

10. Grass to cut | crawl | lawn |

74

Name_____

Directions for the student: **Practice reading 15 aw words on this page.** Choose 2-3 colors. Color *yes* if the sentence makes sense or could possibly be true. Color *no* if it does not make sense or could not be true.

1. A dog dug up the lawn. | yes | no |

2. Get Shawn a straw. | yes | no |

3. The sun sets at dawn. | yes | no |

4. Ben crawls on the lawn. | yes | no |

5. The law lets us speed. | yes | no |

6. I saw a kid with paws. | yes | no |

7. Aw, I hope he gets well. | yes | no |

8. I yawn with my jaw. | yes | no |

9. Dawn's cat has claws. | yes | no |

10. Draw a hat on the man. | yes | no |

Directions for the student: **Practice reading 21 aw words on this page.** Choose 2-3 colors. Read each sentence or phrase. Pick the best answer and color it.

1. A baby deer

| law | fawn |

2. Well-kept grass

| saw | lawn |

3. Meat can be this

| yawn | raw |

4. On dogs

| dawn | paws |

5. On cats

| claws | draw |

6. Dad cuts logs with it.

| saw | jaw |

7. Shawn sucks on it.

| straw | paw |

8. Bugs do it.

| draw | crawl |

9. At sunrise

| dawn | raw |

10. Did see

| saw | law |

Name_____

Directions for the student: **Practice reading 12 aw words on this page.** Choose 2-3 colors. Color *yes* if the sentence makes sense or could possibly be true. Color *no* if it does not make sense or could not be true.

1. Dawn eats straws.	yes	no
2. The cat yawns.	yes	no
3. Cut a tree with a saw.	yes	no
4. This lawn is green.	yes	no
5. Kids eat raw meat.	yes	no
6. Dad crawls to his job.	yes	no
7. Shawn can draw a sun.	yes	no
8. We eat lunch at dawn.	yes	no
9. Mom has claws.	yes	no
10. My jaw is sore.	yes	no

Name_____

Directions for the student: **Practice reading 23 aw words on this page.** Choose 2-3 colors. Read each sentence or phrase. Pick the best answer and color it.

1. Sleepy kids do it.

yawn	lawn

2. Keep off of it.

straw	lawn

3. It can cut logs.

yawn	saw

4. Baby Al will do it.

dawn	crawl

5. On cat's paws

claws	saw

6. Do it on paper

draw	flaw

7. Shawn's is red.

straw	paw

8. Not cooked

law	raw

9. The time Ed gets up.

dawn	shawl

10. It has claws.

yawn	hawk

Name_____

Directions for the student: Color **yes** if the sentence makes sense or could possibly be true. Color **no** if it does not make sense or could not be true.

1. Shawn bent his straw. | yes | no |

2. Aw, a dog's paw is cut. | yes | no |

3. I saw a fawn. | yes | no |

4. Dawn broke the law. | yes | no |

5. Hawks say hee-haw. | yes | no |

Directions for the student: Read each sentence or phrase. Pick the best answer and color it.

6. It is green. | lawn | yawn |

7. Can do it with a pen. | draw | crawl |

8. Shawn's got hit. | claw | jaw |

9. Use to suck up milk. | dawn | straw |

10. Cuts a tree | raw | saw |

Name_____

Directions for the student: **Practice reading 13 au / augh words on this page.** Choose 2-3 colors. Color *yes* if the sentence makes sense or could possibly be true. Color *no* if it does not make sense or could not be true.

1. I caught a tree.	yes	no
2. I taught Pam to do it.	yes	no
3. Dan is naughty.	yes	no
4. It is Paul's fault.	yes	no
5. My daughter is a boy.	yes	no
6. An auto is a car.	yes	no
7. Trucks can haul the sun.	yes	no
8. Paul likes the autumn.	yes	no
9. Laundry tubs are haunted.	yes	no
10. Dad caught a cold.	yes	no

Name_____

Directions for the student: **Practice reading 20 au / augh words on this page.** Choose 2-3 colors. Read each sentence or phrase. Pick the best answer and color it.

1. A bad child	naughty | haunt
2. A summer month	autumn | August
3. A reason for it	cause | pause
4. Mom did it.	haunt | laundry
5. Did teach	caught | taught
6. Trains do this.	laundry | haul
7. A boy's name	fault | Paul
8. A little stop	pause | haunt
9. Mom's girl	cause | daughter
10. Did it to a ball	taught | caught

Name_____

Directions for the student: **Practice reading 11 au / augh words on this page.** Color *yes* if the sentence makes sense or could possibly be true. Color *no* if it does not make sense or could not be true.

1. Mom folds the laundry.

yes	no

2. A match can cause fire.

yes	no

3. It is not his fault.

yes	no

4. Paul caught the fog.

yes	no

5. August is a month.

yes	no

6. Trucks can haul rocks.

yes	no

7. My daughter is a frog.

yes	no

8. Mom taught pigs to eat.

yes	no

9. Pause here for a bit.

yes	no

10. Grass is naughty.

yes	no

Name_____

Directions for the student: **Practice reading 21 au / augh words on this page.** Choose 2-3 colors. Read each sentence or phrase. Pick the best answer and color it.

1. A ghost will do it.

laundry	haunt

2. Mom's girl child

daughter	fault

3. A job for trucks

haul	taught

4. He taught us.

pause	Paul

5. He made a book.

cause	author

6. She did it in class.

August	taught

7. A reason

cause	haunt

8. A little stop

pause	fault

9. Not a good boy

auto	naughty

10. The fall months

autumn	haul

au and **augh** (as in P**au**l and t**augh**t)

Name_____

Directions for the student: **Practice reading 11 au / augh words on this page.** Choose 2-3 colors. Color **yes** if the sentence makes sense or could possibly be true. Color **no** if it does not make sense or could not be true.

1. The crash was his fault. | yes | no |

2. I caught the pond. | yes | no |

3. Pause for a little bit. | yes | no |

4. I met the author. | yes | no |

5. Naughty kids are bad. | yes | no |

6. Ed did the laundry. | yes | no |

7. Ann's daughter is sweet. | yes | no |

8. Pepper causes sneezes. | yes | no |

9. Paul got in his auto. | yes | no |

10. I taught the plant to see. | yes | no |

Name_____

Directions for the student: **Practice reading 21 au / augh words on this page.** Choose 2-3 colors. Read each sentence or phrase. Pick the best answer and color it.

1. A car

auto	caught

2. Showed how

taught	haunt

3. Spooky

haunt	haul

4. Mom did it.

autumn	laundry

5. Why it happened

cause	caught

6. Stop for a bit

pause	haunt

7. To take away

haul	Paul

8. Because of him

fault	autumn

9. Dad's baby girl

daughter	taught

10. To act badly

naughty	author

Name_____

Directions for the student: Color **yes** if the sentence makes sense or could possibly be true. Color **no** if it does not make sense or could not be true.

1. His daughter did laundry. | yes | no |

2. I taught the auto to yell. | yes | no |

3. Paul caught the sun. | yes | no |

4. The author went home. | yes | no |

5. It is his fault. | yes | no |

Directions for the student: Read each sentence or phrase. Pick the best answer and color it.

6. Need soap for it | daughter | laundry |

7. After summer | cause | autumn |

8. Blame | fault | haul |

9. Did catch | taught | caught |

10. Made a mess | pause | naughty |

Name_____

Directions for the student: **Practice reading 13 ew words on this page.** Choose 2-3 colors. Color *yes* if the sentence makes sense or could possibly be true. Color *no* if it does not make sense or could not be true.

1. The plant grew a nose. | yes | no

2. Pam got a new dress. | yes | no

3. Dogs say "mew". | yes | no

4. The pig flew. | yes | no

5. Andrew drew a cat. | yes | no

6. Chew up the tree. | yes | no

7. The wind blew. | yes | no

8. A few kids had stew. | yes | no

9. I threw Dad's van. | yes | no

10. Chew a few nuts. | yes | no

Name_____

Directions for the student: **Practice reading 21 ew words on this page.** Choose 2-3 colors. Read each sentence or phrase. Pick the best answer and color it.

1. Kids did this last year.

stew	grew

2. Not old

new	dew

3. The wind did it.

threw	blew

4. Meat is in it.

pews	stew

5. It came from a desk.

screw	brew

6. A jet did it.

drew	flew

7. Teeth do it.

chew	drew

8. Kittens say it.

mew	grew

9. Not many

flew	few

10. Drew did it to a ball.

threw	brew

Name_____

Directions for the student: **Practice reading 12 ew words on this page.** Choose 2-3 colors. Color *yes* if the sentence makes sense or could possibly be true. Color *no* if it does not make sense or could not be true.

1. We got a new van. | yes | no |

2. Drew flew in the sewer. | yes | no |

3. A few socks slept. | yes | no |

4. Pens can chew. | yes | no |

5. I blew on the hot tea. | yes | no |

6. Mom threw me away. | yes | no |

7. Take a bath in the stew. | yes | no |

8. My feet grew. | yes | no |

9. Cats mew. | yes | no |

10. Dew feels wet. | yes | no |

ew (as in n**ew** or m**ew**)

Name_____

Directions for the student: **Practice reading 22 ew words on this page.** Choose 2-3 colors. Read each sentence or phrase. Pick the best answer and color it.

1. Dad reads it.

screw	news

2. Rain goes in it.

stew	sewer

3. Never used

few	new

4. Do it when you eat.

chew	drew

5. Dad needs a few.

screws	blew

6. Sit on it in church.

sewer	pew

7. May be on the grass

mew	dew

8. Do it to tea.

brew	grew

9. Drew ate it.

screw	stew

10. The plant did it.

grew	flew

ew (as in n**ew** or m**ew**)

Name_____

Directions for the student: **Practice reading 16 ew words on this page.** Choose 2-3 colors. Color *yes* if the sentence makes sense or could possibly be true. Color *no* if it does not make sense or could not be true.

1. The crew did the job. | yes | no |

2. Drew's hat blew off. | yes | no |

3. We did hear the news. | yes | no |

4. Dogs chew screws. | yes | no |

5. Andrew flew his kite. | yes | no |

6. His cat drew a line. | yes | no |

7. Brew tea in a sewer. | yes | no |

8. I ate a few new trucks. | yes | no |

9. The jewel grew. | yes | no |

10. Stew is made of rocks. | yes | no |

Name_____

Directions for the student: **Practice reading 20 ew words on this page.** Choose 2-3 colors. Read each sentence or phrase. Pick the best answer and color it.

1. Got bigger

flew	grew

2. Twist it into wood

mew	screw

3. Beef and veggies

stew	new

4. To crunch and munch

chew	drew

5. Did it to my nose

new	blew

6. Not a lot

brew	few

7. Like a bench

threw	pew

8. Drains a street

sewer	brew

9. Tossed

dew	threw

10. It is on TV.

grew	news

Name_____

Directions for the student: Color **yes** if the sentence makes sense or could possibly be true. Color **no** if it does not make sense or could not be true.

1. Ed grew a new hand. | yes | no |

2. Jill had a few jewels. | yes | no |

3. Tim blew away. | yes | no |

4. Andrew has a new hat. | yes | no |

5. Chew a few rocks. | yes | no |

Directions for the student: Read each sentence or phrase. Pick the best answer and color it.

6. In a street | sewer | jewels |

7. Smell it! | grew | stew |

8. Do it to gum. | brew | chew |

9. A kitten will say it. | mew | flew |

10. Will get grass wet | few | dew |

Name_____

Directions for the student: **Practice reading 19 *a says uh* words on this page.** Choose 2-3 colors. Color ***yes*** if the sentence makes sense or could possibly be true. Color ***no*** if it does not make sense or could not be true.

1. Adults adore bad smells. | yes | no |

2. The alarm woke Emma. | yes | no |

3. Elsa's leg is ashamed. | yes | no |

4. Brenda's nose adores me. | yes | no |

5. Adell agrees with Amanda. | yes | no |

6. Ella will attend church. | yes | no |

7. Linda naps for awhile. | yes | no |

8. Bugs and pigs are alike. | yes | no |

9. Donna can afford that. | yes | no |

10. The map fell asleep. | yes | no |

Name_____

Directions for the student: **Practice reading 20 *a says uh* words on this page.** Choose 2-3 colors. Read each sentence or phrase. Pick the best answer and color it.

1. By myself

again	alone

2. I like what you say.

agree	attend

3. One more time

about	again

4. A grown-up

adult	alone

5. Scared

agree	afraid

6. The same

alike	adopt

7. To go to a meeting

attend	agree

8. Yes, do it.

allow	about

9. Not here

about	away

10. In the past

ago	alive

Name_____

Directions for the student: **Practice reading 23 *a says uh* words on this page.** Choose 2-3 colors. Color *yes* if the sentence makes sense or could possibly be true. Color *no* if it does not make sense or could not be true.

1. Donna is wide awake. | yes | no |

2. Ella is alone again. | yes | no |

3. Brenda is afraid of Linda. | yes | no |

4. The alarm clock ran away. | yes | no |

5. Alaska will amaze Emma. | yes | no |

6. Go along with the adults. | yes | no |

7. I agree to assist Amanda. | yes | no |

8. Let's adopt Adell's leg. | yes | no |

9. Go across the street. | yes | no |

10. We agreed about it. | yes | no |

Name_____

Directions for the student: **Practice reading 21 *a says uh* words on this page.** Choose 2-3 colors. Read each sentence or phrase. Pick the best answer and color it.

1. Not dead

alone	alive

2. Set it to wake you.

alarm	amuse

3. Not with

apart	agree

4. To help

assist	afraid

5. Not awake

adopt	asleep

6. To go with

alive	along

7. A little time

agree	awhile

8. Full of wonder

again	amaze

9. More than I need

extra	away

10. A state

apply	Alaska

Name_____

Directions for the student: **Practice reading 19 *a says uh* words on this page.** Choose 2-3 colors. Color *yes* if the sentence makes sense or could possibly be true. Color *no* if it does not make sense or could not be true.

1. Assist Brenda again. | yes | no |

2. Go along with Linda. | yes | no |

3. I agree to set the alarm. | yes | no |

4. Elsa can afford the sun. | yes | no |

5. Twins are alike. | yes | no |

6. Emma went to Alaska. | yes | no |

7. Donna's dog ran away. | yes | no |

8. The alarm fell asleep. | yes | no |

9. It's about time! | yes | no |

10. We agreed to adopt him. | yes | no |

Name_____

Directions for the student: **Practice reading 23 *a says uh* words on this page.** Choose 2-3 colors. Read each sentence or phrase. Pick the best answer and color it.

1. Amanda set it.

alive	alarm

2. Repeat

alive	again

3. Ask to get a job.

apply	awhile

4. You are right.

awhile	agree

5. Moms and dads

ago	adults

6. Do it to a child.

away	adopt

7. To make smile

amuse	again

8. Left over

extra	amaze

9. Linda's pet is this.

again	asleep

10. Elsa is from here.

apply	Atlanta

Name_____

Directions for the student: Color **yes** if the sentence makes sense or could possibly be true. Color **no** if it does not make sense or could not be true.

1. Donna fell asleep.

yes	no

2. Linda is alone again.

yes	no

3. Amanda amazes me.

yes	no

4. Emma is awake again.

yes	no

5. Kids adopt adults.

yes	no

Directions for the student: Read each sentence or phrase. Pick the best answer and color it.

6. Hide me!

award	afraid

7. The same

alike	ago

8. Yes, yes, yes!

agree	asleep

9. Not a kid

assist	adult

10. Sip it.

adore	cola

Name_____

Directions for the student: **Practice reading 18 all / al words on this page.** Choose 2-3 colors. Color *yes* if the sentence makes sense or could possibly be true. Color *no* if it does not make sense or could not be true.

1. Chalk can talk. | yes | no |

2. Walk in the hall. | yes | no |

3. I take baths at the mall. | yes | no |

4. Call the ball. | yes | no |

5. Tall men are small. | yes | no |

6. I went to a carnival. | yes | no |

7. The horse is in a stall. | yes | no |

8. The corn stalks got tall. | yes | no |

9. Pass the salt to Walter. | yes | no |

10. All walls can walk. | yes | no |

all and **al** (as in w**all** and w**al**k)

Name_____

Directions for the student: **Practice reading 22 all / al words on this page.** Choose 2-3 colors. Read each sentence or phrase. Pick the best answer and color it.

1. To speak

stall	talk

2. It is on chips.

salt	tall

3. Use on a sidewalk.

chalk	hall

4. Can paint it.

walk	wall

5. A boy

talk	Walter

6. Not big

small	fall

7. Shop here.

tall	mall

8. Kids do it.

stalk	talk

9. Not small.

tall	call

10. Do not run. Do this.

hall	walk

Name_____

Directions for the student: **Practice reading 15 all / al words on this page.** Choose 2-3 colors. Color *yes* if the sentence makes sense or could possibly be true. Color *no* if it does not make sense or could not be true.

1. Walter can also go. | yes | no |

2. Jan will trip and fall. | yes | no |

3. Salt the ball. | yes | no |

4. Ben walks to the mall. | yes | no |

5. It is almost time to go. | yes | no |

6. The pan talks to me. | yes | no |

7. Call me if you can. | yes | no |

8. A ball can walk. | yes | no |

9. All kids are tall. | yes | no |

10. Stand by that wall. | yes | no |

Name_____

Directions for the student: **Practice reading 20 all / al words on this page.** Choose 2-3 colors. Read each sentence or phrase. Pick the best answer and color it.

1. Feet do it.

walk	talk

2. Every time

always	wall

3. Little

fall	small

4. Shake it on.

mall	salt

5. Dad is this.

hall	tall

6. Play with it.

call	ball

7. A time of year

fall	hall

8. It can be yellow.

chalk	talk

9. I hear it.

talk	salt

10. Nearly

also	almost

Name_____

Directions for the student: **Practice reading 18 all / al words on this page.** Choose 2-3 colors. Color **yes** if the sentence makes sense or could possibly be true. Color **no** if it does not make sense or could not be true.

1. We walk with feet. | yes | no |

2. A rock will get tall. | yes | no |

3. I always like to fall. | yes | no |

4. Walter is also a girl. | yes | no |

5. All balls are small. | yes | no |

6. Call the wall. | yes | no |

7. Talk to that tall man. | yes | no |

8. Chalk can walk. | yes | no |

9. A leaf falls in the fall. | yes | no |

10. The sun is always hot. | yes | no |

all and al (as in wall and walk)

Name_____

Directions for the student: **Practice reading 24 all / al words on this page.** Choose 2-3 colors. Read each sentence or phrase. Pick the best answer and color it.

1. Walter went here.	fall	mall
2. A horse is in it.	stall	stalk
3. Small kids may do it.	fall	also
4. Mom calls to do it.	chalk	talk
5. Pass it to Walter.	hall	salt
6. Just about	ball	almost
7. Take steps to do it.	walk	small
8. To put it in	install	talk
9. Stop	halt	salt
10. Not upset	malt	calm

Name_____

Directions for the student: Color **yes** if the sentence makes sense or could possibly be true. Color **no** if it does not make sense or could not be true.

1. Salt can talk.

yes	no

2. The ball hit the wall.

yes	no

3. Walter did fall.

yes	no

4. Chalk walks.

yes	no

5. Kids are always tall.

yes	no

Directions for the student: Read each sentence or phrase. Pick the best answer and color it.

6. We walk here.

hall	call

7. Bugs are it.

small	fall

8. Goes with pepper

stall	salt

9. It can be red.

also	ball

10. All kids do it.

wall	talk

Name_____

Directions for the student: **Practice reading 19 nk words on this page.** Choose 2-3 colors. Color *yes* if the sentence makes sense or could possibly be true. Color *no* if it does not make sense or could not be true.

1. Tell the sink thanks.   yes | no

2. Monkeys are pink.   yes | no

3. Frank honks the horn.   yes | no

4. The skunk is drunk.   yes | no

5. A mink coat is soft.   yes | no

6. The ship sank.   yes | no

7. I think I'll drink pink ink.   yes | no

8. Bunk beds stink.   yes | no

9. Skate at a rink.   yes | no

10. Hank blinks.   yes | no

Name_____

Directions for the student: **Practice reading 21 nk words on this page.** Choose 2-3 colors. Read each sentence or phrase. Pick the best answer and color it.

1. A color

mink	pink

2. It can stink.

honk	skunk

3. To say inside of you

rink	think

4. It gets wet.

sink	trunk

5. Skate here.

bunk	rink

6. In a pen

ink	sink

7. To beep a horn

honk	drank

8. Save here.

bank	blink

9. It got smaller.

shrunk	stink

10. Sip it.

drink	blink

Name_____

Directions for the student: **Practice reading 20 nk words on this page.** Choose 2-3 colors. Color *yes* if the sentence makes sense or could possibly be true. Color *no* if it does not make sense or could not be true.

1. Junk is in Hank's trunk. | yes | no

2. Frank fills in the blanks. | yes | no

3. Most men's hair is pink. | yes | no

4. A skunk can flunk. | yes | no

5. A rose stinks. | yes | no

6. Legs can wink and blink. | yes | no

7. Frank dunks feet in ink. | yes | no

8. Skunks kiss monkeys. | yes | no

9. I think my pants shrunk. | yes | no

10. Get a drink at the sink. | yes | no

Name_____

Directions for the student: **Practice reading 21 nk words on this page.** Choose 2-3 colors. Read each sentence or phrase. Pick the best answer and color it.

1. To shut one eye

junk	wink

2. To pull hair hard

yank	bank

3. To not pass a grade

flunk	skunk

4. Went to the bottom

sank	stink

5. Trash it.

junk	think

6. In the back of a car

blink	trunk

7. Beep, beep!

sink	honk

8. Frank did it to milk.

bank	drank

9. At a zoo

bunk	monkey

10. Light red color

rink	pink

Name_____

Directions for the student: **Practice reading 16 nk words on this page.** Choose 2-3 colors. Color *yes* if the sentence makes sense or could possibly be true. Color *no* if it does not make sense or could not be true.

1. Hank's feet stink. | yes | no |

2. Kids rob banks. | yes | no |

3. Vans have blinkers. | yes | no |

4. The bunk shrunk. | yes | no |

5. A bank can think. | yes | no |

6. The monkey is drunk. | yes | no |

7. Pigs have trunks. | yes | no |

8. Frank winks at Jill. | yes | no |

9. A cup is in the sink. | yes | no |

10. I think I will drink milk. | yes | no |

Name_____

Directions for the student: **Practice reading 22 nk words on this page.** Choose 2-3 colors. Read each sentence or phrase. Pick the best answer and color it.

1. On a bunk bed

blanket	honk

2. Stars do it.

bank	twinkle

3. He drank too much.

stink	drunk

4. Will not pass.

flunk	trunk

5. Jim broke his.

pink	ankle

6. Made of ice

blink	rink

7. Wind it up.

crank	blank

8. To dip in milk

bank	dunk

9. Can go up trees.

skunk	monkey

10. Print a name on it.

rink	blank

Name_____

Directions for the student: Color **yes** if the sentence makes sense or could possibly be true. Color **no** if it does not make sense or could not be true.

1. The skunk shrunk.

yes	no

2. A blanket is on a bunk.

yes	no

3. Hank may flunk.

yes	no

4. Frank keeps junk.

yes	no

5. Drink pink ink.

yes	no

Directions for the student: Read each sentence or phrase. Pick the best answer and color it.

6. By a leg

think	ankle

7. Stack 2 beds

bunk	sank

8. A dish is in it.

blink	sink

9. Smells

stinks	pink

10. Do it from a cup

honk	drink

119

Name_____

Directions for the student: **Practice reading 21 ng words on this page.** Choose 2-3 colors. Color *yes* if the sentence makes sense or could possibly be true. Color *no* if it does not make sense or could not be true.

1. Angry cats fling strings.	yes | no
2. Pigs sing long songs.	yes | no
3. Kings have fangs.	yes | no
4. Dogs play ping-pong.	yes | no
5. I hung it on a hanger.	yes | no
6. The bell went ding-dong.	yes | no
7. Chang bangs on a drum.	yes | no
8. Strong lungs take in air.	yes | no
9. Mom cut my long bangs.	yes | no
10. He has a lot of strength.	yes | no

           121

Name_____

Directions for the student: **Practice reading 24 ng words on this page.** Choose 2-3 colors. Read each sentence or phrase. Pick the best answer and color it.

1. Not weak

| lung | strong |

2. On a ladder

| rungs | tongs |

3. With a queen

| bang | king |

4. What you sing

| song | hung |

5. Mad

| angry | long |

6. Birds fly with them.

| bangs | wings |

7. Bees do it.

| sting | song |

8. On the king's finger

| angle | ring |

9. Tie with it.

| fling | string |

10. How long

| length | song |

Name_____

Directions for the student: **Practice reading 18 ng words on this page.** Choose 2-3 colors. Color *yes* if the sentence makes sense or could possibly be true. Color *no* if it does not make sense or could not be true.

1. A ring is on my finger. | yes | no |

2. That is a long song. | yes | no |

3. A fly has wings. | yes | no |

4. The king stung me. | yes | no |

5. His lungs belong to me. | yes | no |

6. A ladder has rungs. | yes | no |

7. Hang up the hangers. | yes | no |

8. Bring me the ring. | yes | no |

9. Wings are made of string. | yes | no |

10. Sting the swing. | yes | no |

Name_____

Directions for the student: **Practice reading 23 ng words on this page.** Choose 2-3 colors. Read each sentence or phrase. Pick the best answer and color it.

1. A bell did it	fang	rang
2. Not right	lung	wrong
3. Strong men have it.	bang	strength
4. Inside of you	string	lungs
5. Do it to a song.	sing	ring
6. I felt this way.	angry	song
7. I do not have them.	lungs	wings
8. A kite needs it.	string	cling
9. Have along with you	bring	rung
10. On a bug	wings	bangs

Name_____

Directions for the student: **Practice reading 17 ng words on this page.** Choose 2-3 colors. Color *yes* if the sentence makes sense or could possibly be true. Color *no* if it does not make sense or could not be true.

#	Sentence	yes	no
1.	Bang with a hammer.	yes	no
2.	That wing stung him.	yes	no
3.	His arm is in a sling.	yes	no
4.	My finger got angry.	yes	no
5.	Birds sing in the spring.	yes	no
6.	A sock is strong.	yes	no
7.	He hung up on me.	yes	no
8.	Cut a length of string.	yes	no
9.	A king slept a long time.	yes	no
10.	I sang the wrong song.	yes	no

      125

Name_____

Directions for the student: **Practice reading 22 ng words on this page.** Choose 2-3 colors. Read each sentence or phrase. Pick the best answer and color it.

1. Jingle Bells

lung	song

2. Can lift a lot.

bang	strong

3. A wolf has them.

wings	fangs

4. In a closet

hangers	bang

5. A train can be it.

cling	long

6. Toss it.

bring	fling

7. We did it at church.

strong	sang

8. For a broken arm

sling	clang

9. How long it is

length	lungs

10. Do with a hammer.

rung	bang

Name_____

Directions for the student: Color **yes** if the sentence makes sense or could possibly be true. Color **no** if it does not make sense or could not be true.

1. A king has wings. | yes | no |

2. The ring stung me. | yes | no |

3. My lungs got angry. | yes | no |

4. Things went wrong. | yes | no |

5. Bring a hanger to mom. | yes | no |

Directions for the student: Read each sentence or phrase. Pick the best answer and color it.

6. The big man is this. | hang | strong |

7. My sister cut them. | bangs | lungs |

8. A wasp did it. | stung | bring |

9. Kids play on them. | long | swings |

10. A bunch of bad men | gang | length |

Name_____

Directions for the student: **Practice reading 21 soft c words on this page.** Choose 2-3 colors. Color *yes* if the sentence makes sense or could possibly be true. Color *no* if it does not make sense or could not be true.

1. Lettuce is like cement. | yes | no

2. This city was once nice. | yes | no

3. The price is ten cents. | yes | no

4. Lance will fix the fence. | yes | no

5. Nancy decides to dance. | yes | no

6. Mice are in the cellar. | yes | no

7. Scissors cut cement. | yes | no

8. Spencer lost the race. | yes | no

9. He fell twice on the ice. | yes | no

10. Cindy ate a slice of pie. | yes | no

Name_____

Directions for the student: **Practice reading 24 soft c words on this page.** Choose 2-3 colors. Read each sentence or phrase. Pick the best answer and color it.

1. On Cindy's collar	lace	prince
2. The middle	center	cent
3. In a jail	face	cell
4. A a big town	dice	city
5. Nancy runs in it.	spice	race
6. Past the sun	space	grace
7. Do it with a pencil.	mice	trace
8. A nose is on it.	dice	face
9. Spencer eats it.	rice	lace
10. Ten in a dime.	nice	cents

Name_____

Directions for the student: **Practice reading 22 soft c words on this page.** Choose 2-3 colors. Color *yes* if the sentence makes sense or could possibly be true. Color *no* if it does not make sense or could not be true.

1. Ice has a lot of spice. | yes | no |

2. Mice take advice. | yes | no |

3. Nancy likes silence. | yes | no |

4. We will practice twice. | yes | no |

5. Trace with a pencil. | yes | no |

6. It's a nice office. | yes | no |

7. Spencer races at recess. | yes | no |

8. Cindy's face will dance. | yes | no |

9. Eat a slice of cement. | yes | no |

10. Peace is nice. | yes | no |

Name_____

Directions for the student: **Practice reading 22 soft c words on this page.** Choose 2-3 colors. Read each sentence or phrase. Pick the best answer and color it.

1. A queen's son	prince	price
2. Nancy is this.	dice	nice
3. Cindy ran fast in it.	race	rice
4. It can taste hot.	spice	city
5. Do it with feet.	dance	rice
6. It is cold.	lace	ice
7. Two times	grace	twice
8. Mom hates them.	mice	cents
9. Dots are on them.	race	dice
10. What it costs	spice	price

132

Name_____

Directions for the student: **Practice reading 22 soft c words on this page.** Choose 2-3 colors. Color *yes* if the sentence makes sense or could possibly be true. Color *no* if it does not make sense or could not be true.

1. Cindy saves me a place.

yes	no

2. Trace this sentence twice.

yes	no

3. Dice are made of ice.

yes	no

4. Dance on the ceiling.

yes	no

5. Nancy went to France.

yes	no

6. I lost my balance on ice.

yes	no

7. Her face costs ten cents.

yes	no

8. Mice are juicy and spicy.

yes	no

9. A fence can race.

yes	no

10. He did cancel the dance.

yes	no

Name_____

Directions for the student: **Practice reading 25 soft c words on this page.** Choose 2-3 colors. Read each sentence or phrase. Pick the best answer and color it.

1. See lions here.

circus	since

2. An apple can be it.

face	juicy

3. It keeps pets in.

fence	space

4. No violence

peace	once

5. To cut

except	slice

6. A job place

office	decent

7. A chance for fun

recess	twice

8. To do well

success	rice

9. Nancy prints with it.

pace	pencil

10. A frozen drip

icicle	acid

Name_____

Directions for the student: Color **yes** if the sentence makes sense or could possibly be true. Color **no** if it does not make sense or could not be true.

1. The prince bit the fence.

yes	no

2. Nancy cancels the race.

yes	no

3. A pencil is in the office.

yes	no

4. The price is ten cents.

yes	no

5. We ate rice and mice.

yes	no

Directions for the student: Read each sentence or phrase. Pick the best answer and color it.

6. For a game

dice	twice

7. In Cindy's glass

grace	ice

8. Lips are on it.

fence	face

9. On a street

cement	space

10. Spencer ate it.

rice	cell

135

Name_____

Directions for the student: **Practice reading 18 soft g words on this page.** Choose 2-3 colors. Color *yes* if the sentence makes sense or could possibly be true. Color *no* if it does not make sense or could not be true.

1. The judge ate fudge. | yes | no |

2. George won the germ. | yes | no |

3. A bridge is in the fridge. | yes | no |

4. Dad's age is six. | yes | no |

5. Angie ran in gym. | yes | no |

6. A giant is huge. | yes | no |

7. Gene has a big badge. | yes | no |

8. Gymnasts sleep in cages. | yes | no |

9. The page has a smudge. | yes | no |

10. We pledge to the flag. | yes | no |

Name_____

Directions for the student: **Practice reading 25 soft g words on this page.** Choose 2-3 colors. Read each sentence or phrase. Pick the best answer and color it.

1. Soap kills it.

badge	germ

2. Gene had fun here.

gel	gym

3. Angie ate it.

fudge	judge

4. How old you are

age	wage

5. In books

gems	pages

6. Huge man

giant	cage

7. Say it to the flag.

edge	pledge

8. Sends men to jail

judge	ledge

9. A giraffe can be in it.

cage	fudge

10. George's pay

wage	stage

Name_____

Directions for the student: **Practice reading 19 soft g words on this page.** Choose 2-3 colors. Color *yes* if the sentence makes sense or could possibly be true. Color *no* if it does not make sense or could not be true.

1. Germs are huge. | yes | no |

2. Angels are stingy. | yes | no |

3. Fudge is orange. | yes | no |

4. Open the large package. | yes | no |

5. The bridge has damage. | yes | no |

6. Angie is gentle. | yes | no |

7. George got the message. | yes | no |

8. Giraffes do magic tricks. | yes | no |

9. Gene fell off the ledge. | yes | no |

10. A cage is for kids. | yes | no |

Soft g and **dge** (as in a**g**e and fu**dge**)

Name_____

Directions for the student: **Practice reading 25 soft g words on this page.** Choose 2-3 colors. Read each sentence or phrase. Pick the best answer and color it.

1. A giant	pledge	huge
2. George pins it on.	badge	page
3. Like candy	fudge	edge
4. Angie acts on it.	age	stage
5. Lock it.	page	cage
6. Can make us sick	pledge	germs
7. On Ginger's cut	bandage	fudge
8. It can fly.	pigeon	judge
9. Sent to Gene	bridge	package
10. Has a big neck	giraffe	gym

140

Soft g and **dge** (as in age and fu**dge**)

Name_____

Directions for the student: **Practice reading 18 soft g words on this page.** Choose 2-3 colors. Color *yes* if the sentence makes sense or could possibly be true. Color *no* if it does not make sense or could not be true.

1. I sent Gene a message. | yes | no |

2. George has energy. | yes | no |

3. The men fix the bridge. | yes | no |

4. A cage is for germs. | yes | no |

5. His luggage is damaged. | yes | no |

6. A package is in storage. | yes | no |

7. We can damage the sun. | yes | no |

8. Angie rips the page. | yes | no |

9. Gerald sat on the ledge. | yes | no |

10. George has allergies. | yes | no |

Name_____

Directions for the student: **Practice reading 21 soft g words on this page.** Choose 2-3 colors. Read each sentence or phrase. Pick the best answer and color it.

1. Glass can be it.	fragile	judge
2. On Gene's jacket	fringe	grudge
3. To get him to do it.	urge	age
4. A color	age	orange
5. A kind of hammer	page	sledge
6. Can be on a gate	hinge	wage
7. It can fly.	stage	pigeon
8. Not little	large	dodge
9. Over a river	bridge	fringe
10. A cop has it.	giraffe	badge

Name_____

Directions for the student: Color **yes** if the sentence makes sense or could possibly be true. Color **no** if it does not make sense or could not be true.

1. Keep fudge in a cage.

yes	no

2. Germs are made of gel.

yes	no

3. His badge is large.

yes	no

4. It is a huge package.

yes	no

5. Gene is on the bridge.

yes	no

Directions for the student: Read each sentence or phrase. Pick the best answer and color it.

6. It has an edge.

page	wage

7. Can get Angie sick

bridge	germs

8. It came in the mail.

ledge	package

9. Ten years old

stage	age

10. George ate it.

huge	orange

143

Name_____

Directions for the student: **Practice reading 12 wr words on this page.** Choose 2-3 colors. Color *yes* if the sentence makes sense or could possibly be true. Color *no* if it does not make sense or could not be true.

1. A wreath can write. | yes | no |

2. A wrench is for a pig. | yes | no |

3. A wrestler hurt his wrist. | yes | no |

4. Tom is wrong. | yes | no |

5. I will wreck the sun. | yes | no |

6. Wring out the wet rag. | yes | no |

7. A wrecker tows a van. | yes | no |

8. Wrap up the gift. | yes | no |

9. The shirt is wrinkled. | yes | no |

10. I wrote Mom a note. | yes | no |

Name_____

Directions for the student: **Practice reading 20 wr words on this page.** Choose 2-3 colors. Read each sentence or phrase. Pick the best answer and color it.

1. Do it with a pen.

wrap	write

2. It bends.

wrote	wrist

3. Has a big, red bow.

wreath	wrench

4. Cars may do it.

wreck	write

5. A tool

wrist	wrench

6. Not right

wrap	wrong

7. Do it to a wet rag.

wrench	wring

8. Men can do it.

wrestle	wrist

9. A dress may do it.

wrinkle	wreath

10. Do it to gifts.

wrap	wreck

Name_____

Directions for the student: **Practice reading 11 kn words on this page.** Choose 2-3 colors. Color **yes** if the sentence makes sense or could possibly be true. Color **no** if it does not make sense or could not be true.

1. Jeff's knuckle bled. | yes | no |

2. Tie a knot. | yes | no |

3. Cut the sun with a knife. | yes | no |

4. I kneel with my knees. | yes | no |

5. Turn the knob to get in. | yes | no |

6. She knit me a hat. | yes | no |

7. Bugs knock on rocks. | yes | no |

8. Tom knew the facts. | yes | no |

9. A knight can fight. | yes | no |

10. That tree knows me. | yes | no |

Name_____

Directions for the student: **Practice reading 22 kn words on this page.** Choose 2-3 colors. Read each sentence or phrase. Pick the best answer and color it.

1. On a hand

knuckle	knee

2. Bend legs to do it.

kneel	knit

3. Tie it.

know	knot

4. Cut with it.

knife	knee

5. A fist can do it.

knock	kneel

6. On a door

knit	knob

7. Known to fight

knight	knit

8. Do it with knees.

knead	kneel

9. A brain's job

knot	know

10. Use yarn to do it.

knock	knit

Name_____

Directions for the student: **Practice reading 10 mb words on this page.** Choose 2-3 colors. Color *yes* if the sentence makes sense or could possibly be true. Color *no* if it does not make sense or could not be true.

1. Plumbers fix vans. | yes | no |

2. Comb hair with a pen. | yes | no |

3. Climb into the pot. | yes | no |

4. Sweep up the crumbs. | yes | no |

5. The tree limb fell. | yes | no |

6. My thumb will sob. | yes | no |

7. He acts dumb. | yes | no |

8. Bombs can kill. | yes | no |

9. A lamb can drive. | yes | no |

10. Climb the hill. | yes | no |

Name_____

Directions for the student: **Practice reading 20 mb words on this page.** Choose 2-3 colors. Read each sentence or phrase. Pick the best answer and color it.

1. Not smart

bomb	dumb

2. Do it to hair.

climb	comb

3. It fell from a tree.

limb	bomb

4. He will fix a leak.

crumbs	plumber

5. On a hand

thumb	climb

6. A baby sheep

lamb	limb

7. Planes drop them.

bombs	combs

8. Go up steps.

crumb	climb

9. Can't feel

numb	lamb

10. From toast

thumbs	crumbs

150

Name_____

Directions for the student: **Practice reading 20 wr/ kn/ mb words on this page.** Choose 2-3 colors. Color *yes* if the sentence makes sense or could possibly be true. Color *no* if it does not make sense or could not be true.

1. I know this top wrinkles. | yes | no |

2. Comb hair with a knife. | yes | no |

3. Lambs can write letters. | yes | no |

4. Tie the plumber in a knot. | yes | no |

5. My knee feels numb. | yes | no |

6. I knew he was wrong. | yes | no |

7. Knit a hat with a wrench. | yes | no |

8. A bomb can wreck things. | yes | no |

9. Knights only eat crumbs. | yes | no |

10. Wring out the door knob. | yes | no |

Name_____

Directions for the student: **Practice reading 21 wr / kn / mb words on this page.** Choose 2-3 colors. Read each sentence or phrase. Pick the best answer and color it.

1. Crushed cloth	wrinkled	dumb
2. A string has it.	climb	knot
3. With a brush	comb	wreath
4. No feeling in it	knock	numb
5. Can do it to pray.	kneel	wrist
6. Twist the wet out	knob	wring
7. On a tree	limbs	knead
8. Did write	wrap	wrote
9. On a leg	knee	bomb
10. It is soft.	knife	lamb

Name_____

Directions for the student: Color **yes** if the sentence makes sense or could possibly be true. Color **no** if it does not make sense or could not be true.

1. Tie combs in knots. | yes | no |

2. Phil knows how to write. | yes | no |

3. A knife can wrinkle. | yes | no |

4. A gopher knits hats. | yes | no |

5. Lambs wrestle dolphins. | yes | no |

Directions for the student: Read each sentence or phrase. Pick the best answer and color it.

6. A plumber has it. | dumb | wrench |

7. Chat on it. | phone | wreck |

8. Did know | numb | knew |

9. In a frame | knock | photo |

10. Bits of cake | crumbs | kneel |

Name_____

Directions for the student: **Practice reading 15 ch sounded /k/ words on this page.** Choose 2-3 colors. Color *yes* if the sentence makes sense or could possibly be true. Color *no* if it does not make sense or could not be true.

1. Chris has a backache. | yes | no |

2. The ship has an anchor. | yes | no |

3. Dogs sing in the choir. | yes | no |

4. Chemicals may harm us. | yes | no |

5. Cats go to school. | yes | no |

6. Christy loves zucchini. | yes | no |

7. I got gifts on Christmas. | yes | no |

8. Chemists mix chemicals. | yes | no |

9. Schedule a stomachache. | yes | no |

10. A sick man had chemo. | yes | no |

Name_____

Directions for the student: **Practice reading 21 ch sounded /k/ words on this page.** Choose 2-3 colors. Read each sentence or phrase. Pick the best answer and color it.

1. Kids go to it.	chemical	school
2. To plan it	schedule	ache
3. For cancer	chemo	choir
4. A holiday	Christmas	tech
5. Sing in it.	Chris	choir
6. Out of control	chaos	anchor
7. Food is in it.	stomach	chrome
8. It hurts.	monarch	ache
9. A squash plant	zucchini	school
10. Uses chemicals	chemist	chord

Name_____

Directions for the student: **Practice reading 11 ch sounded /sh/ words on this page.** Choose 2-3 colors. Color *yes* if the sentence makes sense or could possibly be true. Color *no* if it does not make sense or could not be true.

1. His cat is a chef.

yes	no

2. The frog has a mustache.

yes	no

3. He slid down the chute.

yes	no

4. Fix the machine.

yes	no

5. Dogs play charades.

yes	no

6. Charlotte is late.

yes	no

7. Michelle is from Chicago.

yes	no

8. He trims his mustache.

yes	no

9. Chiffon is a sheer fabric.

yes	no

10. He is from Michigan.

yes	no

Name_____

Directions for the student: **Practice reading 21 ch sounded /sh/ words on this page.** Choose 2-3 colors. Read each sentence or phrase. Pick the best answer and color it.

1. The mitten state | Chicago | Michigan |

2. Flip switch to run | charade | machine |

3. On his top lip | chute | mustache |

4. In a kitchen | chef | parachute |

5. On her dress | chiffon | brochure |

6. A hanging lamp | chute | chandelier |

7. Read it | chef | brochure |

8. A kind of slide | chute | chiffon |

9. To jump from jets | charade | parachute |

10. Charlotte's mom | machine | Michelle |

Name_____

Directions for the student: **Practice reading 20 ch sounded /k/ and /sh/ words on this page.** Choose 2-3 colors. Color *yes* if the sentence makes sense or could possibly be true. Color *no* if it does not make sense or could not be true.

1. The chef made zucchini. | yes | no |

2. A machine can ache. | yes | no |

3. Charlotte went to school. | yes | no |

4. Michelle has a mustache. | yes | no |

5. Stomachs play charades. | yes | no |

6. Find a Chicago brochure. | yes | no |

7. Parachutes need chemo. | yes | no |

8. Schedule a choir to sing. | yes | no |

9. Chemists lick chandeliers. | yes | no |

10. Chris lives in Michigan. | yes | no |

Name_____

Directions for the student: **Practice reading 23 ch sounded /k/ and /sh/ words on this page.** Choose 2-3 colors. Read each sentence or phrase. Pick the best answer and color it.

1. A tech will fix it.

chef	machine

2. It can ache.

stomach	brochure

3. Michelle cooks it.

zucchini	parachute

4. Tells you when

mustache	schedule

5. Cooks meals

chaos	chef

6. Go here to learn.

school	machine

7. Hair on a lip

brochure	mustache

8. Drop from a boat

chiffon	anchor

9. Floats in the sky.

choir	parachute

10. Can be poison

chute	chemicals

Name_____

Directions for the student: Color **yes** if the sentence makes sense or could possibly be true. Color **no** if it does not make sense or could not be true.

1. Michelle is in the choir. | yes | no |

2. A stomach is a machine. | yes | no |

3. His mustache aches. | yes | no |

4. Chris is a chef. | yes | no |

5. Charlotte bit an anchor. | yes | no |

Directions for the student: Read each sentence or phrase. Pick the best answer and color it.

6. Find it on a map. | Michigan | chord |

7. Some stomachs | charades | ache |

8. A ship has it. | mustache | anchor |

9. A chef chops it. | zucchini | chute |

10. Schedule for repair | machine | chaos |

Name_____

Directions for the student: **Practice reading 18 wa words on this page.** Choose 2-3 colors. Color *yes* if the sentence makes sense or could possibly be true. Color *no* if it does not make sense or could not be true.

1. Get water from wands. | yes | no |

2. Swans eat waffles. | yes | no |

3. Swat the wasp! | yes | no |

4. I will swallow the swamp. | yes | no |

5. A watch can walk. | yes | no |

6. Walt has a wad of gum. | yes | no |

7. Wanda wants to be sick. | yes | no |

8. Wallets are for wasps. | yes | no |

9. Ducks waddle. | yes | no |

10. I will wash the dish. | yes | no |

Name_____

Directions for the student: **Practice reading 23 wa words on this page.** Choose 2-3 colors. Read each sentence or phrase. Pick the best answer and color it.

1. Do it to water. | swallow | swat |

2. A fairy has it. | wasp | wand |

3. Wet land | swamp | swan |

4. Wanda sips it. | wall | water |

5. Do it to hands. | walk | wash |

6. Wish to have | want | wasp |

7. Tell time with it. | swab | watch |

8. Walt's feet will do it. | waffle | walk |

9. It swims. | swan | wall |

10. It can sting. | wasp | want |

Name_____

Directions for the student: **Practice reading 19 wa words on this page.** Choose 2-3 colors. Color **yes** if the sentence makes sense or could possibly be true. Color **no** if it does not make sense or could not be true.

1. Swans use wands.

yes	no

2. I want to eat that wall.

yes	no

3. We wash waffles.

yes	no

4. Wasps waddle.

yes	no

5. Wanda kills the wasp.

yes	no

6. Walt wads up the paper.

yes	no

7. Watch me!

yes	no

8. Kids sleep in swamps.

yes	no

9. Walnuts want to walk.

yes	no

10. Swallow the water.

yes	no

Name_____

Directions for the student: **Practice reading 23 wa words on this page.** Choose 2-3 colors. Read each sentence or phrase. Pick the best answer and color it.

1. On a wrist	watch	wad
2. Do it in the tub.	wash	walk
3. Hope to get	want	wasp
4. We all need it.	wander	water
5. To hit	swan	swat
6. Frogs are here.	swab	swamp
7. I want to eat them.	waffles	wasps
8. Wanda will wash it.	want	wall
9. A bug that can fly	wasp	waltz
10. Gets us wet.	walnut	water

Name_____

Directions for the student: **Practice reading 18 wa words on this page.** Choose 2-3 colors. Color *yes* if the sentence makes sense or could possibly be true. Color *no* if it does not make sense or could not be true.

1. My dog made waffles.

yes	no

2. Trees walk and waddle.

yes	no

3. He wants to wash up.

yes	no

4. Watch me do a waltz.

yes	no

5. I will swallow the wall.

yes	no

6. Wanda pets the wasp.

yes	no

7. I want a glass of water.

yes	no

8. Swamp water is wet.

yes	no

9. Walt lost his wallet.

yes	no

10. My watch is old.

yes	no

Name_____

Directions for the student: **Practice reading 23 wa words on this page.** Choose 2-3 colors. Read each sentence or phrase. Pick the best answer and color it.

1. Ducks do it.

waddle	wasp

2. Water is in it.

swat	swamp

3. Wanda bit it.

walnut	swan

4. A happy yell

wahoo	wad

5. A fairy has it.

wand	swab

6. In a home

swamp	walls

7. Do it to water.

swallow	walk

8. Can be in a pocket.

wallet	waltz

9. Add soap to it.

wasp	washer

10. A kind of dance

waltz	wand

Name_____

Directions for the student: Color **yes** if the sentence makes sense or could possibly be true. Color **no** if it does not make sense or could not be true.

1. Wash the wasp.

yes	no

2. Swallow the wallet.

yes	no

3. Walk on walnuts.

yes	no

4. It was a big wall.

yes	no

5. Swans hate water.

yes	no

Directions for the student: Read each sentence or phrase. Pick the best answer and color it.

6. Gets us wet

wasp	water

7. Not a run

walk	wad

8. Wish to get

swamp	want

9. Made of bricks

wallet	wall

10. Get mud off

wash	wand

Name_____

Directions for the student: **Practice reading 12 war words on this page.** Choose 2-3 colors. Color *yes* if the sentence makes sense or could possibly be true. Color *no* if it does not make sense or could not be true.

1. I had warts on my hand. | yes | no

2. A warden is at a jail. | yes | no

3. Snow is warm. | yes | no

4. I warn you not to do it. | yes | no

5. Pigs go to war. | yes | no

6. Jill ran toward Tim. | yes | no

7. Warren got an award. | yes | no

8. Warn them of the dog. | yes | no

9. Dwarfs can warp. | yes | no

10. His reward is candy. | yes | no

Name_____

Directions for the student: **Practice reading 20 war words on this page.** Choose 2-3 colors. Read each sentence or phrase. Pick the best answer and color it.

1. Ugly bump on skin	war	wart
2. Bent out of shape	warn	warp
3. Not cold	warden	warm
4. A big fight	ward	war
5. A man's name	wart	Warren
6. Do not do it.	warning	award
7. His job is in a jail.	warden	warm
8. Clothes	wardrobe	ward
9. You can win it.	wart	award
10. To go nearer	toward	Warren

Name_____

Directions for the student: **Practice reading 12 war words on this page.** Choose 2-3 colors. Color *yes* if the sentence makes sense or could possibly be true. Color *no* if it does not make sense or could not be true.

1. Dust is an award. | yes | no |

2. The coward ran away. | yes | no |

3. Socks warm my feet. | yes | no |

4. Warn the swarm of bees. | yes | no |

5. The cups had a war. | yes | no |

6. Warren came toward us. | yes | no |

7. I fell backward. | yes | no |

8. Rocks get warts. | yes | no |

9. A plane can fly upward. | yes | no |

10. Fire has warmth. | yes | no |

Name_____

Directions for the student: **Practice reading 22 war words on this page.** Choose 2-3 colors. Read each sentence or phrase. Pick the best answer and color it.

1. The sun gives it.	award	warmth
2. Men can die in it.	war	warp
3. Not backward	wart	forward
4. He is not brave.	coward	warm
5. Kites go this way.	warden	upward
6. A prize	warp	award
7. A job in a jail	warden	toward
8. Danger!	warning	award
9. A bunch of bees	swarm	warm
10. On Warren's hand	wart	dwarf

Name_____

Directions for the student: **Practice reading 12 war words on this page.** Choose 2-3 colors. Color *yes* if the sentence makes sense or could possibly be true. Color *no* if it does not make sense or could not be true.

1. Warren ate a warm sock. | yes | no |

2. Warn him to keep out. | yes | no |

3. All cowards get warts. | yes | no |

4. Freeze to get warm. | yes | no |

5. Kids must go to war. | yes | no |

6. He will win an award. | yes | no |

7. A swarm of bees came. | yes | no |

8. That van went backward. | yes | no |

9. Trees warn us. | yes | no |

10. A dwarf is not big. | yes | no |

Name_____

Directions for the student: **Practice reading 22 war words on this page.** Choose 2-3 colors. Read each sentence or phrase. Pick the best answer and color it.

1. Watch out!

reward	warning

2. Not forward

backward	warden

3. Small person

inward	dwarf

4. Kill or get killed

war	warm

5. To come closer

warp	toward

6. For being best

award	war

7. Has keys to cells

warden	toward

8. Blankets are it.

warn	warm

9. Not downward

awkward	upward

10. For doing well

swarm	reward

Name_____

Directions for the student: Color **yes** if the sentence makes sense or could possibly be true. Color **no** if it does not make sense or could not be true.

1. Warts win awards. | yes | no |

2. Get warmth from fire. | yes | no |

3. I will warn the warden. | yes | no |

4. Cowards win awards. | yes | no |

5. Warren came toward us. | yes | no |

Directions for the student: Read each sentence or phrase. Pick the best answer and color it.

6. Heat | dwarf | warmth |

7. Be careful. | warning | warp |

8. For a good job | swarm | reward |

9. Rise | upward | war |

10. Not brave | warden | coward |

Name_____

Directions for the student: **Practice reading 13 wor words on this page.** Choose 2-3 colors. Color *yes* if the sentence makes sense or could possibly be true. Color *no* if it does not make sense or could not be true.

1. The worst is the best. | yes | no

2. A worm has on socks. | yes | no

3. A cat works at a job. | yes | no

4. The world is little. | yes | no

5. His car is worth a lot. | yes | no

6. He worships God. | yes | no

7. A worm can say words. | yes | no

8. The worker got worse. | yes | no

9. Do not worry at work. | yes | no

10. Birds eat worms. | yes | no

Name_____

Directions for the student: **Practice reading 20 wor words on this page.** Choose 2-3 colors. Read each sentence or phrase. Pick the best answer and color it.

1. Fish bite them.

work	worms

2. Not as good

worse	work

3. Can do it to God.

worship	worm

4. Read them.

worse	words

5. It has land on it.

world	words

6. It is in your mind.

worry	worms

7. Get paid to do this.

worse	work

8. How much value

worth	worst

9. A man doing a job

worm	worker

10. Most awful

worst	word

wor (as in **wor**m)

Name_____

Directions for the student: **Practice reading 11 wor words on this page.** Choose 2-3 colors. Color **yes** if the sentence makes sense or could possibly be true. Color **no** if it does not make sense or could not be true.

1. I can read the words. | yes | no

2. A car is worth a dime. | yes | no

3. The world fits in a box. | yes | no

4. Worms worship God. | yes | no

5. I had work to do. | yes | no

6. Dan had the worst test. | yes | no

7. The workers dug a hole. | yes | no

8. Feed words to the pigs. | yes | no

9. I worry about him. | yes | no

10. Worms eat vans. | yes | no

Name_____

Directions for the student: **Practice reading 20 wor words on this page.** Choose 2-3 colors. Read each sentence or phrase. Pick the best answer and color it.

1. Say them.

words	worse

2. We are on it.

word	world

3. Men do it.

work	worm

4. Do it in your mind.

worse	worry

5. See it in the dirt.

work	worm

6. Men on a job

workers	worth

7. The most bad

worship	worst

8. How much

worth	world

9. Praise to God

worry	worship

10. A job

work	worse

Name_____

Directions for the student: **Practice reading 12 wor words on this page.** Choose 2-3 colors. Color **yes** if the sentence makes sense or could possibly be true. Color **no** if it does not make sense or could not be true.

1. Bugs worry about worms. | yes | no |

2. The workers went to work. | yes | no |

3. The world is big. | yes | no |

4. Words can swim. | yes | no |

5. The workers will fix it. | yes | no |

6. Dogs eat worms. | yes | no |

7. This pain is the worst. | yes | no |

8. He did his work. | yes | no |

9. I worry about the test. | yes | no |

10. Gold is worth a lot. | yes | no |

Name_____

Directions for the student: **Practice reading 21 wor words on this page.** Choose 2-3 colors. Read each sentence or phrase. Pick the best answer and color it.

#	Sentence/Phrase	Option 1	Option 2
1.	Cannot worry	worker	worm
2.	We live here.	world	worse
3.	Do it on a job	work	worth
4.	Lips say them.	worry	words
5.	The most awful	worst	worm
6.	Fear it will happen	worry	worth
7.	In mom's garden	words	worms
8.	He gets paid.	world	worker
9.	Sing to God	worry	worship
10.	Print them.	worse	words

Name_____

Directions for the student: Color **yes** if the sentence makes sense or could possibly be true. Color **no** if it does not make sense or could not be true.

1. Worms hug dolls. | yes | no |

2. The workers work hard. | yes | no |

3. Dust off the world. | yes | no |

4. Hogs worship kids. | yes | no |

5. Words worry. | yes | no |

Directions for the student: Read each sentence or phrase. Pick the best answer and color it.

6. This planet | word | world |

7. Fear | worry | work |

8. The most bad | worst | worth |

9. Spell them | words | worse |

10. He will do work. | world | worker |

   185

Name_____

Directions for the student: **Practice reading 10 ed words on this page.** Choose 2-3 colors. Color *yes* if the sentence makes sense or could possibly be true. Color *no* if it does not make sense or could not be true.

1. He's excited to see me. | yes | no |

2. Tom handed me the sun. | yes | no |

3. We tested math skills. | yes | no |

4. Dan wasted paper. | yes | no |

5. Mom heated the mop. | yes | no |

6. I braided Jen's nose. | yes | no |

7. The book ended sadly. | yes | no |

8. Jane and Tim dated. | yes | no |

9. I parted my hair. | yes | no |

10. Jim loaded up the truck. | yes | no |

Name_____

Directions for the student: **Practice reading 20 ed words on this page.** Choose 2-3 colors. Read each sentence or phrase. Pick the best answer and color it.

1. Broken

busted	listed

2. Lots and lots

ragged	crowded

3. Very smart

gifted	ended

4. Fur can be it.

blasted	matted

5. Jump up and down

noted	excited

6. Lots of trees

pitted	wooded

7. Throws a lot out

wasted	banded

8. A ship did it.

landed	minded

9. Bent up

sided	crooked

10. Just skin

naked	spotted

ed (as in fix**ed** and fri**ed**)

Name_____

Directions for the student: **Practice reading 10 ed words on this page.** Choose 2-3 colors. Color **yes** if the sentence makes sense or could possibly be true. Color **no** if it does not make sense or could not be true.

1. Sam cracked the nuts. | yes | no |

2. Mom plugged the tub. | yes | no |

3. We fixed the bug's hair. | yes | no |

4. The rock loved the cat. | yes | no |

5. Jim failed the test. | yes | no |

6. A masked man broke in. | yes | no |

7. We fried mud for lunch. | yes | no |

8. He killed the sun. | yes | no |

9. My leg dried up. | yes | no |

10. I checked my homework. | yes | no |

Name_____

Directions for the student: **Practice reading 22 ed words on this page.** Choose 2-3 colors. Read each sentence or phrase. Pick the best answer and color it.

1. Sick, but got well	mixed	cured
2. At an end	finished	dressed
3. Made to do it	fried	forced
4. Did not pass	failed	raked
5. Crushed into bits	filed	smashed
6. Husband and wife	married	plugged
7. Pretended	killed	faked
8. Got the wet off	dried	planned
9. Tore it	picked	ripped
10. Need sleep	tired	brushed

Name_____

Directions for the student: **Practice reading 20 ed words on this page.** Choose 2-3 colors. Color **yes** if the sentence makes sense or could possibly be true. Color **no** if it does not make sense or could not be true.

1. I'm tired of braided hair. | yes | no

2. Mom heated fried ham. | yes | no

3. I hated that he got killed. | yes | no

4. I picked a spotted cat. | yes | no

5. The spoiled kid cried. | yes | no

6. I ripped the top I loved. | yes | no

7. He dated a caged bird. | yes | no

8. An excited kid raced. | yes | no

9. I loved how it ended. | yes | no

10. We fixed a cracked dish. | yes | no

ed (as in test**ed**, fix**ed**, and fri**ed**)

Name_____

Directions for the student: **Practice reading 20 ed words on this page.** Choose 2-3 colors. Read each sentence or phrase. Pick the best answer and color it.

1. Did it to grass

braided	raked

2. A dog can be this.

married	spotted

3. He did it to a gun.

boiled	loaded

4. A store did this.

landed	closed

5. Ann and Al did it.

dated	caged

6. Glass was this.

cracked	naked

7. Brother and sister

ripped	related

8. Can't get in.

locked	pitted

9. Did it with hands.

cried	clapped

10. Set on a hot stove

mixed	heated

Name_____

Directions for the student: Color **yes** if the sentence makes sense or could possibly be true. Color **no** if it does not make sense or could not be true.

1. My dog dated a cat.

yes	no

2. We raked the cake.

yes	no

3. The toy excited Jim.

yes	no

4. Ben raced and won.

yes	no

5. My desk cried.

yes	no

Directions for the student: Read each sentence or phrase. Pick the best answer and color it.

6. Took a life

gifted	killed

7. Old clothes

ragged	raged

8. Had to have it

needed	pressed

9. Did it for a trip

packed	tested

10. Ate chips

dated	snacked

193

Name_____

Directions for the student: **Practice reading 11 final -al words on this page.** Choose 2-3 colors. Color **yes** if the sentence makes sense or could possibly be true. Color **no** if it does not make sense or could not be true.

1. An oval is a shape. | yes | no |

2. A rental car is for trips. | yes | no |

3. Sam is in the hospital. | yes | no |

4. The final test was hard. | yes | no |

5. His cat went on trial. | yes | no |

6. Dan's arrival was late. | yes | no |

7. Tammy lost a sandal. | yes | no |

8. My journal is personal. | yes | no |

9. Bugs get medals. | yes | no |

10. That video went viral. | yes | no |

Name_____

Directions for the student: **Practice reading 20 final -al words on this page.** Choose 2-3 colors. Read each sentence or phrase. Pick the best answer and color it.

1. Okay with the law	legal	oval

2. Near here	local	moral

3. Add an "s" to words	bridal	plural

4. Print in it.	medal	journal

5. The last or the end	final	rental

6. On feet	sandals	total

7. The "big" letters	capitals	floral

8. In the mind	mental	fatal

9. When he gets here	arrival	sandal

10. If someone dies	fatal	dental

Name_____

Directions for the student: **Practice reading 22 final –le words on this page.** Choose 2-3 colors. Color **yes** if the sentence makes sense or could possibly be true. Color **no** if it does not make sense or could not be true.

1. He lit the purple candle. | yes | no |

2. My uncle cuddles beetles. | yes | no |

3. Little turtles eat pickles. | yes | no |

4. Mom is able to handle it. | yes | no |

5. A rifle gets pimples. | yes | no |

6. Make a single circle. | yes | no |

7. A rattle is in the cradle. | yes | no |

8. Ankles twinkle. | yes | no |

9. Cattle sing Jingle Bells. | yes | no |

10. Drizzle makes puddles. | yes | no |

Name_____

Directions for the student: **Practice reading 22 final –le words on this page.** Choose 2-3 colors. Read each sentence or phrase. Pick the best answer and color it.

1. No wife or husband | pebbles | single |

2. Easy | purple | simple |

3. Splash in it. | puddle | tickle |

4. On a pan | handle | mumble |

5. A sock is on it. | single | ankle |

6. Fun to do | tremble | puzzle |

7. On a belt | buckle | cripple |

8. Can do it. | ripple | able |

9. Has a shell. | bundle | turtle |

10. Snuggle | single | cuddle |

Name_____

Directions for the student: **Practice reading 21 final –le words on this page.** Choose 2-3 colors. Color *yes* if the sentence makes sense or could possibly be true. Color *no* if it does not make sense or could not be true.

1. Hospitals fix rattles.	yes	no
2. Turtles win medals.	yes	no
3. Six people wore sandals.	yes	no
4. My uncle handles a rifle.	yes	no
5. A traffic signal is purple.	yes	no
6. A pickle went on trial.	yes	no
7. The manual has a title.	yes	no
8. A local floral shop closed.	yes	no
9. I finally got the total.	yes	no
10. Saddles are for cattle.	yes	no

al and **le** (as in fin**al** and hand**le**)

Name_____

Directions for the student: **Practice reading 21 final –le words on this page.** Choose 2-3 colors. Read each sentence or phrase. Pick the best answer and color it.

1. Not mine to keep

rental	pebbles

2. On top of feet

ankles	moral

3. More than one

plural	tickle

4. Not for a man

rattle	sandal

5. An egg shape

oval	drizzle

6. Buds and petals

paddle	floral

7. Red is to stop.

signal	cripple

8. Do it to a seat belt.

final	buckle

9. B, A, P, G, S, R

turtles	capitals

10. I did step on it.

pebble	hospital

Name_____

Directions for the student: Color **yes** if the sentence makes sense or could possibly be true. Color **no** if it does not make sense or could not be true.

1. People go to funerals.

yes	no

2. A sandal is for an ankle.

yes	no

3. That is an oval table.

yes	no

4. Turtles go to hospitals.

yes	no

5. His uncle is special.

yes	no

Directions for the student: Read each sentence or phrase. Pick the best answer and color it.

6. On a belt

buckle	sandal

7. The end

tackle	final

8. A bug

signal	beetle

9. Splash in it

puddle	scandal

10. A kind of party

pickle	festival

Name_____

Directions for the student: **Practice reading 10 tion words on this page.** Choose 2-3 colors. Color *yes* if the sentence makes sense or could possibly be true. Color *no* if it does not make sense or could not be true.

1. The U.S.A. is a nation. | yes | no

2. Here is our train station. | yes | no

3. Rats go on vacation. | yes | no

4. Pigs can do fractions. | yes | no

5. Kim sits in section five. | yes | no

6. Dan mentions it to Ed. | yes | no

7. That location is near us. | yes | no

8. It is a temptation to lie. | yes | no

9. A bone can do actions. | yes | no

10. Bugs do subtraction. | yes | no

Name_____

Directions for the student: **Practice reading 20 tion words on this page.** Choose 2-3 colors. Read each sentence or phrase. Pick the best answer and color it.

1. A made-up story	lotion	fiction
2. Have fun on it.	vacation	action
3. Tell it.	mention	motion
4. It's on my hands.	fraction	lotion
5. Ten plus ten	station	addition
6. Be careful.	caution	action
7. To feel mad	emotion	motions
8. Trains stop here.	stations	fraction
9. The U.S.A.	nation	action
10. Vote in it.	election	location

Name_____

Directions for the student: **Practice reading 10 sion words on this page.** Choose 2-3 colors. Color **yes** if the sentence makes sense or could possibly be true. Color **no** if it does not make sense or could not be true.

1. Rats own televisions. | yes | no |

2. I made the best decision. | yes | no |

3. His mission is to get rich. | yes | no |

4. Get permission from Dad. | yes | no |

5. Check the frog's vision. | yes | no |

6. It was a big explosion. | yes | no |

7. Find the extension cord. | yes | no |

8. Pay admission to get in. | yes | no |

9. A mansion is little. | yes | no |

10. Ken's passion is art. | yes | no |

sion (as in ses**sion** and ver**sion**)

Name_____

Directions for the student: **Practice reading 20 sion words on this page.** Choose 2-3 colors. Read each sentence or phrase. Pick the best answer and color it.

1. Ask it.

| vision | permission |

2. Kids need it.

| confusion | supervision |

3. Math

| discussion | division |

4. On his face

| expression | mission |

5. His side of it

| version | tension |

6. A goal

| omission | mission |

7. Pay to go in.

| session | admission |

8. Watch it.

| television | persuasion |

9. A big house

| confusion | mansion |

10. Your sight

| division | vision |

Name_____

Directions for the student: **Practice reading 11 cian words on this page.** Choose 2-3 colors. Color *yes* if the sentence makes sense or could possibly be true. Color *no* if it does not make sense or could not be true.

1. Electricians can fix fans. | yes | no |

2. Pediatricians help kids. | yes | no |

3. Beauticians are morticians. | yes | no |

4. My dog is a physician. | yes | no |

5. Musicians cut hair. | yes | no |

6. Politicians have beliefs. | yes | no |

7. A mathematician can add. | yes | no |

8. Dieticians study foods. | yes | no |

9. Technicians hug trees. | yes | no |

10. Opticians provide glasses. | yes | no |

Name_____

Directions for the student: **Practice reading 20 cian words on this page.** Choose 2-3 colors. Read each sentence or phrase. Pick the best answer and color it.

1. Plans meals	optician	dietician
2. Elect them.	politicians	beautician
3. For kids	mortician	pediatrician
4. Does tricks	magician	optician
5. Does funerals	mortician	politician
6. For the sick	optician	physician
7. Cuts hair	electrician	beautician
8. Fixes computers	physician	technician
9. Plays music	musician	magician
10. Does wiring	electrician	pediatrician

Name_____

Directions for the student: **Practice reading 18 tion / sion / cian words on this page.** Choose 2-3 colors. Color **yes** if the sentence makes sense or could possibly be true. Color **no** if it does not make sense or could not be true.

1. Politicians are in elections. | yes | no |

2. A television station is on. | yes | no |

3. Electricians use caution. | yes | no |

4. Physicians make decisions. | yes | no |

5. A mansion needs lotion. | yes | no |

6. Beauticians hate vacations. | yes | no |

7. Opticians check vision. | yes | no |

8. Mathematicians do fractions. | yes | no |

9. Frogs ask permission. | yes | no |

10. Rocks have emotions. | yes | no |

Name_____

Directions for the student: **Practice reading 20 tion / sion / cian words on this page.** Choose 2-3 colors.
Read each sentence or phrase. Pick the best answer and color it.

1. Get gas here.

musician	station

2. A car crash

collision	location

3. Gives you pills.

confusion	physician

4. May get shocks

mention	electrician

5. Turn it on.

television	addition

6. A trip for fun

vacation	decision

7. For the rich

nation	mansion

8. Give to help

donation	passion

9. Part of a whole

tension	fraction

10. Plans menus

dietician	vision

Name_____

Directions for the student: Color **yes** if the sentence makes sense or could possibly be true. Color **no** if it does not make sense or could not be true.

1. Opticians help with vision.

yes	no

2. Find the television station.

yes	no

3. I had permission to go.

yes	no

4. Politicians make decisions.

yes	no

5. Weeds have emotion.

yes	no

Directions for the student: Read each sentence or phrase. Pick the best answer and color it.

6. Happen to say

mention	mortician

7. One fifth

fraction	mission

8. A big, big home

optician	mansion

9. Rub onto skin

tension	lotion

10. Did tricks

nation	magician

tive (as in cap**tive**)

Name_____

Directions for the student: **Practice reading 11 tive words on this page.** Choose 2-3 colors. Color *yes* if the sentence makes sense or could possibly be true. Color *no* if it does not make sense or could not be true.

1. Artists are creative. | yes | no |

2. He is disruptive in class. | yes | no |

3. Most pigs are imaginative. | yes | no |

4. His relative is a detective. | yes | no |

5. Talkative kids are silent. | yes | no |

6. A fugitive runs from cops. | yes | no |

7. That girl is attractive. | yes | no |

8. Rocks are active. | yes | no |

9. A crash is destructive. | yes | no |

10. I am positive he did it. | yes | no |

Name_____

Directions for the student: **Practice reading 20 tive words on this page.** Choose 2-3 colors. Read each sentence or phrase. Pick the best answer and color it.

1. A train

locomotive	native

2. It works well.

effective	divisive

3. A party is it.

addictive	festive

4. Again and again

primitive	repetitive

5. Chats a lot

talkative	positive

6. Helps others

cooperative	captive

7. Keep from harm

protective	active

8. Things get done

productive	vindictive

9. Works well

excessive	effective

10. Stands out

distinctive	collective

Name_____

Directions for the student: **Practice reading 10 sive words on this page.** Choose 2-3 colors. Color *yes* if the sentence makes sense or could possibly be true. Color *no* if it does not make sense or could not be true.

1. Explosives blow things up. | yes | no |

2. Glue is an adhesive. | yes | no |

3. Hens write in cursive. | yes | no |

4. A rat is a massive animal. | yes | no |

5. The painting is impressive. | yes | no |

6. A bunny is repulsive. | yes | no |

7. His hat is abusive. | yes | no |

8. The facts are conclusive. | yes | no |

9. Jon is a decisive person. | yes | no |

10. That toy is inexpensive. | yes | no |

Name_____

Directions for the student: **Practice reading 21 sive words on this page.** Choose 2-3 colors. Read each sentence or phrase. Pick the best answer and color it.

1. Cheap | inexpensive | festive |

2. Makes it stick | adhesive | defensive |

3. Offensive | repulsive | exclusive |

4. Blows up stuff | cursive | explosive |

5. For sure | responsive | decisive |

6. Far-reaching | expansive | expensive |

7. Won't give it | possessive | massive |

8. Hard to catch | divisive | elusive |

9. One of a kind | excessive | exclusive |

10. Stands out | impressive | cursive |

Name_____

Directions for the student: **Practice reading 10 tive and sive words on this page.** Choose 2-3 colors. Color *yes* if the sentence makes sense or could possibly be true. Color *no* if it does not make sense or could not be true.

1. Drugs can be addictive.

yes	no

2. Attentive people nap.

yes	no

3. Hold the sun captive.

yes	no

4. That dog is protective.

yes	no

5. She used excessive glue.

yes	no

6. Ann's skin is sensitive.

yes	no

7. That car is expensive.

yes	no

8. Al is possessive of toys.

yes	no

9. Smelly feet are offensive.

yes	no

10. Robbers are invasive.

yes	no

tive and **sive** (as in cap**tive** and cur**sive**)

Name_____

Directions for the student: **Practice reading 20 tive and sive words on this page.** Choose 2-3 colors. Read each sentence or phrase. Pick the best answer and color it.

1. A lot got done	elusive	productive
2. List in order	decisive	consecutive
3. Kids are this.	active	expansive
4. Held prisoner	captive	intensive
5. Attacks are it.	positive	aggressive
6. Aunts or uncles	relatives	repulsive
7. Too much	native	excessive
8. Huge	massive	negative
9. Convincing	festive	persuasive
10. Sad	motive	depressive

Name_____

Directions for the student: Color **yes** if the sentence makes sense or could possibly be true. Color **no** if it does not make sense or could not be true.

1. Gramps is in intensive care.	yes	no
2. Adjectives are descriptive.	yes	no
3. That show is informative.	yes	no
4. A bug is creative.	yes	no
5. Rocks can be massive.	yes	no

Directions for the student: Read each sentence or phrase. Pick the best answer and color it.

6. Not negative	festive	positive
7. Way of writing	abusive	cursive
8. Costs too much	expensive	subversive
9. It works well.	effective	motive
10. Lies	deceptive	inactive

Name_____

Directions for the student: **Practice reading 10 ture words on this page.** Choose 2-3 colors. Color *yes* if the sentence makes sense or could possibly be true. Color *no* if it does not make sense or could not be true.

1. Cops capture bad men. | yes | no |

2. Take my picture. | yes | no |

3. The future is the past. | yes | no |

4. Moisture makes it damp. | yes | no |

5. The sun is a creature. | yes | no |

6. Sam has good posture. | yes | no |

7. Plants are part of nature. | yes | no |

8. You can puncture a rock. | yes | no |

9. Eggs go on adventures. | yes | no |

10. The fixture is broken. | yes | no |

Name_____

Directions for the student: **Practice reading 20 ture words on this page.** Choose 2-3 colors. Read each sentence or phrase. Pick the best answer and color it.

1. How it feels

texture	culture

2. A cow is here.

lecture	pasture

3. Nose and lips

features	venture

4. Animals

creatures	posture

5. Next year

mature	future

6. To poke a hole

puncture	nature

7. Damp or wet

moisture	rapture

8. Smile for it

mixture	picture

9. Stand up tall

posture	torture

10. Fake teeth

adventure	dentures

Name_____

Directions for the student: **Practice reading 10 sure words on this page.** Choose 2-3 colors. Color *yes* if the sentence makes sense or could possibly be true. Color *no* if it does not make sense or could not be true.

1. Measure the sugar. | yes | no |

2. A box feels pleasure. | yes | no |

3. A rock lost its composure. | yes | no |

4. I'm unsure of the truth. | yes | no |

5. Dad insured our van. | yes | no |

6. Leisure means work time. | yes | no |

7. Dogs are in the enclosure. | yes | no |

8. I assure you, I'm fine. | yes | no |

9. Our tire lost pressure. | yes | no |

10. Bugs hide treasure. | yes | no |

Name_____

Directions for the student: **Practice reading 20 sure words on this page.** Choose 2-3 colors. Read each sentence or phrase. Pick the best answer and color it.

1. Free time	leisure	fissure

2. Gold or riches	pressure	treasure

3. To convince	assure	composure

4. Rub off	pleasure	erasure

5. Fenced in	pressure	enclosure

6. Check amount	measure	reassure

7. Pay to protect	insure	composure

8. Delight	pleasure	fissure

9. Under a force	pressure	assure

10. Not certain	unsure	closure

Name_____

Directions for the student: **Practice reading 13 ture and sure words on this page.** Choose 2-3 colors. Color *yes* if the sentence makes sense or could possibly be true. Color *no* if it does not make sense or could not be true.

1. Ed enjoys his leisure time. | yes | no

2. Vultures take pictures. | yes | no

3. Measure how tall I am. | yes | no

4. Capture the dentures. | yes | no

5. A tantrum is immature. | yes | no

6. Dust is a great treasure. | yes | no

7. Dan fractured his arm. | yes | no

8. Teacher made an erasure. | yes | no

9. Cars are manufactured. | yes | no

10. Dan is under pressure. | yes | no

Name_____

Directions for the student: **Practice reading 20 ture and sure words on this page.** Choose 2-3 colors. Read each sentence or phrase. Pick the best answer and color it.

1. Not positive of it

| pasture | unsure |

2. Little

| miniature | insure |

3. Found outside

| nature | ensure |

4. Draw or color it.

| exposure | picture |

5. A cage

| enclosure | denture |

6. Fun, relaxing times

| leisure | mixture |

7. Candy can give it.

| pleasure | torture |

8. Tires can get them.

| punctures | assure |

9. You can trust me.

| reassure | future |

10. How you stand

| treasure | posture |

Name_____

Directions for the student: Color **yes** if the sentence makes sense or could possibly be true. Color **no** if it does not make sense or could not be true.

1. The temperature is hot. | yes | no |

2. Cats draw good pictures. | yes | no |

3. I'm unsure of what to do. | yes | no |

4. Dust the furniture. | yes | no |

5. Use a ruler to measure. | yes | no |

Directions for the student: Read each sentence or phrase. Pick the best answer and color it.

6. Good feelings | posture | pleasure |

7. Find and send to jail | closure | capture |

8. Teach by telling | lecture | enclosure |

9. May be yes or no | unsure | vulture |

10. Going away | torture | departure |

ANSWER KEY - WORKBOOK B

Page 1	Page 2	Page 3	Page 4	Page 5	Page 6
1. no	1. bread	1. no	1. thread	1. yes	1. bread
2. yes	2. healthy	2. no	2. heavy	2. no	2. sweat
3. no	3. instead	3. no	3. leather	3. no	3. heavy
4. no	4. head	4. yes	4. dead	4. no	4. weather
5. no	5. weapon	5. no	5. breakfast	5. yes	5. meant
6. yes	6. breath	6. yes	6. sweater	6. yes	6. dread
7. no	7. ready	7. no	7. sweat	7. yes	7. head
8. no	8. thread	8. yes	8. bread	8. yes	8. weapon
9. yes	9. heavy	9. no	9. head	9. no	9. death
10. no	10. breath	10. yes	10. feather	10. no	10. leather

Page 7	Page 9	Page 10	Page 11	Page 12	Page 13
1. no	1. yes	1. thief	1. yes	1. veil	1. no
2. no	2. yes	2. field	2. no	2. eight	2. yes
3. yes	3. yes	3. priest	3. yes	3. weigh	3. yes
4. no	4. yes	4. brief	4. no	4. neighbor	4. no
5. no	5. no	5. brownie	5. yes	5. veins	5. yes
6. dead	6. yes	6. niece	6. yes	6. freight	6. yes
7. wealth	7. yes	7. grief	7. yes	7. sleigh	7. no
8. feather	8. yes	8. believe	8. no	8. reigns	8. yes
9. sweat	9. yes	9. cookies	9. yes	9. weight	9. yes
10. read	10. no	10. bootie	10. yes	10. reindeer	10. no

Page 14	Page 15	Page 16	Page 17	Page 18	Page 19
1. conceited	1. yes	1. cookies	1. yes	1. thief	1. no
2. deceives	2. yes	2. ceiling	2. yes	2. neighbor	2. no
3. receive	3. no	3. brownies	3. yes	3. receipt	3. no
4. conceive	4. no	4. deceive	4. no	4. movie	4. yes
5. receipt	5. yes	5. thief	5. no	5. eighty	5. yes
6. ceiling	6. yes	6. veil	6. no	6. deceive	6. brief
7. deceit	7. no	7. movies	7. no	7. Lassie	7. eight
8. receipt	8. yes	8. eighteen	8. yes	8. freight	8. receipt
9. conceive	9. no	9. nightie	9. yes	9. receive	9. veil
10. ceiling	10. no	10. sleigh	10. no	10. eight	10. deceive

Page 21	Page 22	Page 23	Page 24	Page 25	Page 26
1. no	1. point	1. yes	1. poison	1. yes	1. foil
2. yes	2. toilet	2. yes	2. moist	2. no	2. noise
3. yes	3. oil	3. no	3. coin	3. no	3. coil
4. no	4. moist	4. yes	4. boil	4. yes	4. voice
5. yes	5. soil	5. yes	5. soil	5. no	5. boil
6. yes	6. boil	6. no	6. coins	6. yes	6. spoil
7. yes	7. coin	7. no	7. oil	7. yes	7. joint
8. no	8. poison	8. no	8. toilet	8. yes	8. coins
9. yes	9. join	9. no	9. noise	9. no	9. toilet
10. no	10. noise	10. no	10. point	10. yes	10. poison

ANSWER KEY - WORKBOOK B, continued

Page 27	Page 29	Page 30	Page 31	Page 32	Page 33
1. no	1. no	1. joy	1. yes	1. annoy	1. yes
2. no	2. yes	2. toys	2. yes	2. boys	2. yes
3. yes	3. yes	3. annoy	3. no	3. employ	3. yes
4. yes	4. no	4. employ	4. no	4. voyage	4. no
5. no	5. yes	5. royal	5. no	5. tomboy	5. no
6. foil	6. yes	6. boy	6. yes	6. loyal	6. yes
7. coins	7. yes	7. toy	7. yes	7. enjoy	7. yes
8. soil	8. yes	8. loyal	8. no	8. destroy	8. yes
9. poison	9. no	9. soy	9. yes	9. toy	9. yes
10. oink	10. yes	10. destroy	10. yes	10. joyful	10. yes

Page 34	Page 35	Page 37	Page 38	Page 39	Page 40
1. employ	1. no	1. no	1. down	1. no	1. clown
2. boys	2. yes	2. no	2. drown	2. yes	2. frown
3. destroy	3. yes	3. yes	3. towel	3. no	3. shower
4. enjoy	4. yes	4. yes	4. now	4. yes	4. now
5. annoy	5. no	5. yes	5. frown	5. yes	5. brown
6. Roy	6. enjoy	6. yes	6. brown	6. no	6. tower
7. toy	7. toys	7. yes	7. growl	7. no	7. owl
8. loyal	8. voyage	8. no	8. crown	8. yes	8. gown
9. voyage	9. royalty	9. yes	9. cow	9. no	9. allow
10. joyful	10. destroy	10. yes	10. flower	10. yes	10. plow

Page 41	Page 42	Page 43	Page 45	Page 46	Page 47
1. no	1. towel	1. no	1. no	1. mouse	1. no
2. no	2. drowsy	2. no	2. yes	2. couch	2. yes
3. no	3. cow	3. no	3. yes	3. pound	3. yes
4. yes	4. allow	4. yes	4. no	4. house	4. no
5. yes	5. power	5. yes	5. yes	5. mouth	5. no
6. no	6. flowers	6. how	6. no	6. cloud	6. no
7. no	7. owl	7. flowers	7. no	7. round	7. no
8. yes	8. gown	8. frown	8. no	8. sound	8. no
9. no	9. crowd	9. brown	9. yes	9. proud	9. yes
10. yes	10. crown	10. now	10. no	10. blouse	10. no

Page 48	Page 49	Page 50	Page 51	Page 53	Page 54
1. loud	1. no	1. cloud	1. yes	1. yes	1. thought
2. count	2. no	2. house	2. yes	2. no	2. rough
3. proud	3. no	3. ground	3. yes	3. yes	3. dough
4. ground	4. yes	4. couch	4. no	4. no	4. bought
5. sour	5. yes	5. mouse	5. no	5. yes	5. though
6. ouch	6. no	6. loud	6. ground	6. yes	6. brought
7. out	7. no	7. ouch	7. scour	7. no	7. through
8. mouth	8. yes	8. mouth	8. cloud	8. yes	8. enough
9. cloud	9. no	9. sour	9. blouse	9. yes	9. fought
10. found	10. yes	10. blouse	10. pound	10. yes	10. cough

230

ANSWER KEY - WORKBOOK B, continued

Page 55	Page 56	Page 57	Page 58	Page 59	Page 61
1. no	1. drought	1. no	1. enough	1. yes	1. yes
2. yes	2. bough	2. yes	2. dough	2. no	2. no
3. no	3. plough	3. no	3. cough	3. yes	3. yes
4. yes	4. tough	4. yes	4. through	4. no	4. no
5. yes	5. enough	5. yes	5. drought	5. yes	5. no
6. yes	6. bought	6. no	6. ought	6. through	6. yes
7. no	7. thought	7. yes	7. brought	7. bought	7. no
8. yes	8. through	8. no	8. rough	8. thought	8. yes
9. yes	9. doughnut	9. yes	9. sought	9. enough	9. no
10. yes	10. sought	10. yes	10. bought	10. although	10. no

Page 62	Page 63	Page 64	Page 65	Page 66	Page 67
1. pool	1. yes	1. broom	1. yes	1. cook	1. yes
2. tooth	2. yes	2. snooze	2. yes	2. book	2. yes
3. noon	3. yes	3. pool	3. yes	3. wood	3. yes
4. moon	4. no	4. noon	4. no	4. cookie	4. yes
5. room	5. no	5. poop	5. no	5. shook	5. yes
6. zoo	6. no	6. boots	6. yes	6. hood	6. no
7. food	7. no	7. soon	7. yes	7. look	7. yes
8. shoot	8. yes	8. drool	8. yes	8. stood	8. yes
9. cool	9. no	9. spoon	9. yes	9. wood	9. no
10. choose	10. no	10. tooth	10. yes	10. crook	10. no

Page 68	Page 69	Page 70	Page 71	Page 73	Page 74
1. good	1. no	1. cool	1. no	1. yes	1. paws
2. shook	2. no	2. wood	2. yes	2. no	2. straw
3. book	3. no	3. pool	3. yes	3. yes	3. crawl
4. hood	4. yes	4. groom	4. no	4. yes	4. dawn
5. foot	5. yes	5. zoom	5. no	5. yes	5. draw
6. stood	6. no	6. good	6. hood	6. yes	6. jaw
7. cookie	7. no	7. shook	7. zoom	7. yes	7. saw
8. hook	8. yes	8. hook	8. stool	8. no	8. claw
9. crook	9. yes	9. roof	9. cook	9. yes	9. yawn
10. brook	10. yes	10. cook	10. book	10. yes	10. lawn

Page 75	Page 76	Page 77	Page 78	Page 79	Page 81
1. yes	1. fawn	1. no	1. yawn	1. yes	1. no
2. yes	2. lawn	2. yes	2. lawn	2. yes	2. yes
3. no	3. raw	3. yes	3. saw	3. yes	3. yes
4. yes	4. paws	4. yes	4. crawl	4. yes	4. yes
5. no	5. claws	5. no	5. claws	5. no	5. no
6. no	6. saw	6. no	6. draw	6. lawn	6. yes
7. yes	7. straw	7. yes	7. straw	7. draw	7. no
8. yes	8. crawl	8. no	8. raw	8. jaw	8. yes
9. yes	9. dawn	9. no	9. dawn	9. straw	9. no
10. yes	10. saw	10. yes	10. hawk	10. saw	10. yes

231

Page 82	Page 83	Page 84	Page 85	Page 86	Page 87
1. naughty	1. yes	1. haunt	1. yes	1. auto	1. yes
2. autumn	2. yes	2. daughter	2. no	2. taught	2. no
3. cause	3. yes	3. haul	3. yes	3. haunt	3. no
4. laundry	4. no	4. Paul	4. yes	4. laundry	4. yes
5. taught	5. yes	5. author	5. yes	5. cause	5. yes
6. haul	6. yes	6. taught	6. yes	6. pause	6. laundry
7. Paul	7. no	7. cause	7. yes	7. haul	7. autumn
8. pause	8. no	8. pause	8. yes	8. fault	8. fault
9. daughter	9. yes	9. naughty	9. yes	9. daughter	9. caught
10. caught	10. no	10. autumn	10. no	10. naughty	10. naughty

Page 89	Page 90	Page 91	Page 92	Page 93	Page 94
1. no	1. grew	1. yes	1. news	1. yes	1. grew
2. yes	2. new	2. no	2. sewer	2. yes	2. screw
3. no	3. blew	3. no	3. new	3. yes	3. stew
4. no	4. stew	4. no	4. chew	4. no	4. chew
5. yes	5. screw	5. yes	5. screws	5. yes	5. blew
6. no	6. flew	6. no	6. pew	6. no	6. few
7. yes	7. chew	7. no	7. dew	7. no	7. pew
8. yes	8. mew	8. yes	8. brew	8. no	8. sewer
9. no	9. few	9. yes	9. stew	9. no	9. threw
10. yes	10. threw	10. yes	10. grew	10. no	10. news

Page 95	Page 97	Page 98	Page 99	Page 100	Page 101
1. no	1. no	1. alone	1. yes	1. alive	1. yes
2. yes	2. yes	2. agree	2. yes	2. alarm	2. yes
3. no	3. no	3. again	3. yes	3. apart	3. yes
4. yes	4. no	4. adult	4. no	4. assist	4. no
5. no	5. yes	5. afraid	5. yes	5. asleep	5. yes
6. sewer	6. yes	6. alike	6. yes	6. along	6. yes
7. stew	7. yes	7. attend	7. yes	7. awhile	7. yes
8. chew	8. no	8. allow	8. no	8. amaze	8. no
9. mew	9. yes	9. away	9. yes	9. extra	9. yes
10. dew	10. no	10. ago	10. yes	10. Alaska	10. yes

Page 102	Page 103	Page 105	Page 106	Page 107	Page 108
1. alarm	1. yes	1. no	1. talk	1. yes	1. walk
2. again	2. yes	2. yes	2. salt	2. yes	2. always
3. apply	3. yes	3. no	3. chalk	3. no	3. small
4. agree	4. yes	4. no	4. wall	4. yes	4. salt
5. adults	5. no	5. no	5. Walter	5. yes	5. tall
6. adopt	6. afraid	6. yes	6. small	6. no	6. ball
7. amuse	7. alike	7. yes	7. mall	7. yes	7. fall
8. extra	8. agree	8. yes	8. talk	8. no	8. chalk
9. asleep	9. adult	9. yes	9. tall	9. no	9. talk
10. Atlanta	10. cola	10. no	10. walk	10. yes	10. almost

Page 109	Page 110	Page 111	Page 113	Page 114	Page 115
1. yes	1. mall	1. no	1. no	1. pink	1. yes
2. no	2. stall	2. yes	2. no	2. skunk	2. yes
3. no	3. fall	3. yes	3. yes	3. think	3. no
4. no	4. talk	4. no	4. no	4. sink	4. no
5. no	5. salt	5. no	5. yes	5. rink	5. no
6. no	6. almost	6. hall	6. yes	6. ink	6. no
7. yes	7. walk	7. small	7. no	7. honk	7. no
8. no	8. install	8. salt	8. no	8. bank	8. no
9. yes	9. halt	9. ball	9. yes	9. shrunk	9. yes
10. yes	10. calm	10. talk	10. yes	10. drink	10. yes

Page 116	Page 117	Page 118	Page 119	Page 121	Page 122
1. wink	1. yes	1. blanket	1. no	1. no	1. strong
2. yank	2. no	2. twinkle	2. yes	2. no	2. rungs
3. flunk	3. yes	3. drunk	3. yes	3. no	3. king
4. sank	4. no	4. flunk	4. yes	4. no	4. song
5. junk	5. no	5. ankle	5. no	5. yes	5. angry
6. trunk	6. no	6. rink	6. ankle	6. yes	6. wings
7. honk	7. no	7. crank	7. bunk	7. yes	7. sting
8. drank	8. yes	8. dunk	8. sink	8. yes	8. ring
9. monkey	9. yes	9. monkey	9. stinks	9. yes	9. string
10. pink	10. yes	10. blank	10. drink	10. yes	10. length

Page 123	Page 124	Page 125	Page 126	Page 127	Page 129
1. yes	1. rang	1. yes	1. song	1. no	1. no
2. yes	2. wrong	2. no	2. strong	2. no	2. yes
3. yes	3. strength	3. yes	3. fangs	3. no	3. yes
4. no	4. lungs	4. no	4. hangers	4. yes	4. yes
5. no	5. sing	5. yes	5. long	5. yes	5. yes
6. yes	6. angry	6. no	6. fling	6. strong	6. yes
7. yes	7. wings	7. yes	7. sang	7. bangs	7. no
8. yes	8. string	8. yes	8. sling	8. stung	8. yes
9. no	9. bring	9. yes	9. length	9. swings	9. yes
10. no	10. wings	10. yes	10. bang	10. gang	10. yes

Page 130	Page 131	Page 132	Page 133	Page 134	Page 135
1. lace	1. no	1. prince	1. yes	1. circus	1. no
2. center	2. no	2. nice	2. yes	2. juicy	2. yes
3. cell	3. yes	3. race	3. no	3. fence	3. yes
4. city	4. yes	4. spice	4. no	4. peace	4. yes
5. race	5. yes	5. dance	5. yes	5. slice	5. no
6. space	6. yes	6. ice	6. yes	6. office	6. dice
7. trace	7. yes	7. twice	7. no	7. recess	7. ice
8. face	8. no	8. mice	8. no	8. success	8. face
9. rice	9. no	9. dice	9. no	9. pencil	9. cement
10. cents	10. yes	10. price	10. yes	10. icicle	10. rice

Page 137	Page 138	Page 139	Page 140	Page 141	Page 142
1. yes	1. germ	1. no	1. huge	1. yes	1. fragile
2. no	2. gym	2. no	2. badge	2. yes	2. fringe
3. no	3. fudge	3. no	3. fudge	3. yes	3. urge
4. no	4. age	4. yes	4. stage	4. no	4. orange
5. yes	5. pages	5. yes	5. cage	5. yes	5. sledge
6. yes	6. giant	6. yes	6. germs	6. yes	6. hinge
7. yes	7. pledge	7. yes	7. bandage	7. no	7. pigeon
8. no	8. judge	8. no	8. pigeon	8. yes	8. large
9. yes	9. cage	9. yes	9. package	9. yes	9. bridge
10. yes	10. wage	10. no	10. giraffe	10. yes	10. badge

Page 143	Page 145	Page 146	Page 147	Page 148	Page 149
1. no	1. no	1. write	1. yes	1. knuckle	1. no
2. no	2. no	2. wrist	2. yes	2. kneel	2. no
3. yes	3. yes	3. wreath	3. no	3. knot	3. no
4. yes	4. yes	4. wreck	4. yes	4. knife	4. yes
5. yes	5. no	5. wrench	5. yes	5. knock	5. yes
6. page	6. yes	6. wrong	6. yes	6. knob	6. no
7. germs	7. yes	7. wring	7. no	7. knight	7. yes
8. package	8. yes	8. wrestle	8. yes	8. kneel	8. yes
9. age	9. yes	9. wrinkle	9. yes	9. know	9. no
10. orange	10. yes	10. wrap	10. no	10. knit	10. yes

Page 150	Page 151	Page 152	Page 153	Page 155	Page 156
1. dumb	1. yes	1. wrinkled	1. no	1. yes	1. school
2. comb	2. no	2. knot	2. yes	2. yes	2. schedule
3. limb	3. no	3. comb	3. no	3. no	3. chemo
4. plumber	4. no	4. numb	4. no	4. yes	4. Christmas
5. thumb	5. yes	5. kneel	5. no	5. no	5. choir
6. lamb	6. yes	6. wring	6. wrench	6. yes	6. chaos
7. bombs	7. no	7. limbs	7. phone	7. yes	7. stomach
8. climb	8. yes	8. wrote	8. knew	8. yes	8. ache
9. numb	9. no	9. knee	9. photo	9. no	9. zucchini
10. crumbs	10. no	10. lamb	10. crumbs	10. yes	10. chemist

Page 157	Page 158	Page 159	Page 160	Page 161	Page 163
1. no	1. Michigan	1. yes	1. machine	1. yes	1. no
2. no	2. machine	2. no	2. stomach	2. no	2. no
3. yes	3. mustache	3. yes	3. zucchini	3. no	3. yes
4. yes	4. chef	4. no	4. schedule	4. yes	4. no
5. no	5. chiffon	5. no	5. chef	5. no	5. no
6. yes	6. chandelier	6. yes	6. school	6. Michigan	6. yes
7. yes	7. brochure	7. no	7. mustache	7. ache	7. no
8. yes	8. chute	8. yes	8. anchor	8. anchor	8. no
9. yes	9. parachute	9. no	9. parachute	9. zucchini	9. yes
10. yes	10. Michelle	10. yes	10. chemicals	10. machine	10. yes

Page 164	Page 165	Page 166	Page 167	Page 168	Page 169
1. swallow	1. no	1. watch	1. no	11. waddle	1. no
2. wand	2. no	2. wash	2. no	12. swamp	2. no
3. swamp	3. no	3. want	3. yes	13. walnut	3. no
4. water	4. no	4. water	4. yes	14. wahoo	4. yes
5. wash	5. yes	5. swat	5. no	15. wand	5. no
6. want	6. yes	6. swamp	6. no	16. walls	6. water
7. watch	7. yes	7. waffles	7. yes	17. swallow	7. walk
8. walk	8. no	8. wall	8. yes	18. wallet	8. want
9. swan	9. no	9. wasp	9. yes	19. washer	9. wall
10. wasp	10. yes	10. water	10. yes	20. waltz	10. wash

Page 171	Page 172	Page 173	Page 174	Page 175	Page 176
1. yes	1. wart	11. no	1. warmth	1. no	1. warning
2. yes	2. warp	12. yes	2. war	2. yes	2. backward
3. no	3. warm	13. yes	3. forward	3. no	3. dwarf
4. yes	4. war	14. no	4. coward	4. no	4. war
5. no	5. Warren	15. no	5. upward	5. no	5. toward
6. yes	6. warning	16. yes	6. award	6. yes	6. award
7. yes	7. warden	17. yes	7. warden	7. yes	7. warden
8. yes	8. wardrobe	18. no	8. warning	8. yes	8. warm
9. no	9. award	19. yes	9. swarm	9. no	9. upward
10. yes	10. toward	20. yes	10. wart	10. yes	10. reward

Page 177	Page 179	Page 180	Page 181	Page 182	Page 183
1. no	1. no	1. worms	1. yes	1. words	1. no
2. yes	2. no	2. worse	2. no	2. world	2. yes
3. yes	3. no	3. worship	3. no	3. work	3. yes
4. no	4. no	4. words	4. no	4. worry	4. no
5. yes	5. yes	5. world	5. yes	5. worm	5. yes
6. warmth	6. yes	6. worry	6. yes	6. workers	6. no
7. warning	7. no	7. work	7. yes	7. worst	7. yes
8. reward	8. yes	8. worth	8. no	8. worth	8. yes
9. upward	9. yes	9. worker	9. yes	9. worship	9. yes
10. coward	10. yes	10. worst	10. no	10. work	10. yes

Page 184	Page 185	Page 187	Page 188	Page 189	Page 190
1. worm	1. no	1. yes	1. busted	1. yes	1. cured
2. world	2. yes	2. no	2. crowded	2. yes	2. finished
3. work	3. no	3. yes	3. gifted	3. no	3. forced
4. words	4. no	4. yes	4. matted	4. no	4. failed
5. worst	5. no	5. no	5. excited	5. yes	5. smashed
6. worry	6. world	6. no	6. wooded	6. yes	6. married
7. worms	7. worry	7. yes	7. wasted	7. no	7. faked
8. worker	8. worst	8. yes	8. landed	8. no	8. dried
9. worship	9. words	9. yes	9. crooked	9. no	9. ripped
10. words	10. worker	10. yes	10. naked	10. yes	10. tired

Page 191	Page 192	Page 193	Page 195	Page 196	Page 197
1. yes	1. raked	1. no	1. yes	1. legal	1. yes
2. yes	2. spotted	2. no	2. yes	2. local	2. no
3. yes	3. loaded	3. yes	3. yes	3. plural	3. no
4. yes	4. closed	4. yes	4. yes	4. journal	4. yes
5. yes	5. dated	5. no	5. no	5. final	5. no
6. yes	6. cracked	6. killed	6. yes	6. sandals	6. yes
7. no	7. related	7. ragged	7. yes	7. capitals	7. yes
8. yes	8. locked	8. needed	8. yes	8. mental	8. no
9. yes	9. clapped	9. packed	9. no	9. arrival	9. no
10. yes	10. heated	10. snacked	10. yes	10. fatal	10. yes

Page 198	Page 199	Page 200	Page 201	Page 203	Page 204
1. single	1. no	1. rental	1. yes	1. yes	1. fiction
2. simple	2. no	2. ankles	2. no	2. yes	2. vacation
3. puddle	3. yes	3. plural	3. yes	3. no	3. mention
4. handle	4. yes	4. rattle	4. no	4. no	4. lotion
5. ankle	5. no	5. oval	5. yes	5. yes	5. addition
6. puzzle	6. no	6. floral	6. buckle	6. yes	6. caution
7. buckle	7. yes	7. signal	7. final	7. yes	7. emotion
8. able	8. yes	8. buckle	8. beetle	8. yes	8. stations
9. turtle	9. yes	9. capitals	9. puddle	9. no	9. nation
10. cuddle	10. no	10. pebble	10. festival	10. no	10. election

Page 205	Page 206	Page 207	Page 208	Page 209	Page 210
1. no	1. permission	1. yes	1. dietician	1. yes	1. station
2. yes	2. supervision	2. yes	2. politicians	2. yes	2. collision
3. yes	3. division	3. no	3. pediatrician	3. yes	3. physician
4. yes	4. expression	4. no	4. magician	4. yes	4. electrician
5. no	5. version	5. no	5. mortician	5. no	5. television
6. yes	6. mission	6. yes	6. physician	6. no	6. vacation
7. yes	7. admission	7. yes	7. beautician	7. yes	7. mansion
8. yes	8. television	8. yes	8. technician	8. yes	8. donation
9. no	9. mansion	9. no	9. musician	9. no	9. fraction
10. yes	10. vision	10. yes	10. electrician	10. no	10. dietician

Page 211	Page 213	Page 214	Page 215	Page 216	Page 217
1. yes	1. yes	1. locomotive	1. yes	1. inexpensive	1. yes
2. yes	2. yes	2. effective	2. yes	2. adhesive	2. no
3. yes	3. no	3. festive	3. no	3. repulsive	3. no
4. yes	4. yes	4. repetitive	4. no	4. explosive	4. yes
5. no	5. no	5. talkative	5. yes	5. decisive	5. yes
6. mention	6. yes	6. cooperative	6. no	6. expansive	6. yes
7. fraction	7. yes	7. protective	7. no	7. possessive	7. yes
8. mansion	8. no	8. productive	8. yes	8. elusive	8. yes
9. lotion	9. yes	9. effective	9. yes	9. exclusive	9. yes
10. magician	10. yes	10. distinctive	10. yes	10. impressive	10. yes

Page 218	Page 219	Page 221	Page 222	Page 223	Page 224
1. productive	1. yes	1. yes	1. texture	1. yes	1. leisure
2. consecutive	2. yes	2. yes	2. pasture	2. no	2. treasure
3. active	3. yes	3. no	3. features	3. no	3. assure
4. captive	4. no	4. yes	4. creatures	4. yes	4. erasure
5. aggressive	5. yes	5. no	5. future	5. yes	5. enclosure
6. relatives	6. positive	6. yes	6. puncture	6. no	6. measure
7. excessive	7. cursive	7. yes	7. moisture	7. yes	7. insure
8. massive	8. expensive	8. no	8. picture	8. yes	8. pleasure
9. persuasive	9. effective	9. no	9. posture	9. yes	9. pressure
10. depressive	10. deceptive	10. yes	10. dentures	10. no	10. unsure

Page 225	Page 226	Page 227
1. yes	1. unsure	1. yes
2. no	2. miniature	2. no
3. yes	3. nature	3. yes
4. no	4. picture	4. yes
5. yes	5. enclosure	5. yes
6. no	6. leisure	6. pleasure
7. yes	7. pleasure	7. capture
8. yes	8. punctures	8. lecture
9. yes	9. reassure	9. unsure
10. yes	10. posture	10. departure

Phonics Practice
Made Easy and Fun

Student Workbook A

Includes the following sounds or sound groupings:

Short Vowels
Short a (as in c**a**t)
Short e (as in p**e**t)
Short i (as in s**i**t)
Short o (as in n**o**t)
Short u (as in c**u**p)

Long Vowels
Long a_e (as in **ate**)
Long ai (as in p**ai**n)
Long ay (as in s**ay**)
Long ee (as in k**ee**p)
Long ea (as in t**ea**m)
Long vowel y and ey (as in lad**y** and k**ey**)
Long i_e and ie (as in t**i**m**e** and p**ie**)
Long igh (as in t**igh**t)
Long vowel y (as in tr**y**)
Long o_e and oe (as in j**o**k**e** and t**oe**)
Long oa (as in b**oa**t)
Long ow (as in l**ow**)
Long u_e and ue (as in t**u**b**e**, **use**, **and** bl**ue**)
Long ui (as in s**ui**t)

Consonant Digraphs
sh (as in di**sh**)
th (voiced and unvoiced, as in **th**at and **th**in)
ch and tch (as in **ch**ip and i**tch**)
wh (as in **wh**en)
ph (as in gra**ph**)

R-controlled Vowels
ar (as in c**ar** and c**ar**ry)
er (as in h**er** and v**er**y)
ir (as in st**ir**)
or (as in f**or**t)
ur (as in t**ur**n)

Made in the USA
Columbia, SC
14 July 2022

63391469R10135